In the Valley
of the Gods

In the Valley
of the Gods

Journals of an
American Buddhist
in Nepal

Stephen Clorfeine

Stephen Clorfeine

STATION HILL

BARRYTOWN. LTD.

Published by Station Hill / Barrytown, Ltd. in Barrytown, New York 12507.
E-mail: publishers@stationhill.org
Online catalogue: http://www.stationhill.org

Station Hill Arts is a project of The Institute for Publishing Arts, Inc., a not-for-profit, federally tax exempt organization in Barrytown, New York, which gratefully acknowledges ongoing support for its publishing program from the New York State Council on the Arts.

Back cover photograph of author by Lauren Casalino; all other photographs, including the cover, by Stephen Clorfeine
Maps on pages 11 and 148-149 by Barbara Bash

Cover and text typesetting and design by Susan Quasha

Library of Congress Cataloging-in-Publication Data

Clorfeine, Stephen.
     In the valley of the Gods : journals of an American Buddhist in
     Nepal / Stephen Clorfeine.
        p. cm.
     ISBN 1-58177-061-8 (alk. paper)
        1. Clorfeine, Stephen—Diaries. 2. Buddhists—United States—
     Diaries. 3. Clorfeine, Stephen—Journeys—Nepal. 4. Spiritual
     life—Buddhism—Nepal. 5. Nepal—Religious life. I. Title.
     BQ948.O77 A3 2000
     294.3'092—dc21
     [B]
                                                                00-064192

Manufactured in the United States of America

Contents

Acknowledgments

This book, while focused on my experience as a Buddhist practitioner in Nepal, is about the land and people of Nepal, and my first gratitude is to the people I encountered, their openness and their resilience. It's remarkable that a country like Nepal exists, given the volatile changes in traditional cultures this last half century. And Nepal, balanced geographically and culturally between vast and rapid materialistic forces, edging into complex transitions, retains a spirit that has much to offer the Western seeker. Acknowledging this spirit is first and foremost.

Naropa University gave me the first opportunity to visit and live in Nepal. Venerable Thrangu Rinpoche, along with the senior lamas of his monastery, Lama Sherab, and Lama Ajo, and the nuns of Tara Abbey, touched my heart over and over again on the pilgrimage to Yolmo. I am grateful to all my traveling companions, and particularly to Wendell Beavers in 1999 and Lauren Casalino in 1995.

My friendship with long-time residents of the Kathmandu Valley, Keith Dowman and Joanna Claire, among others, inspired and encouraged me. Several books offered similar support: Ruth Higbie's, *A Classful of Gods and Goddesses in Nepal*, and Peter Mathiessen's, *The Snow Leopard*, and *East of Lo Manthang*.

Steve Gorn was my first and steady collaborator, developing the spoken word and music performances and the CD's which comprise the first two chapters of this book. We worked together over a period of three years, performing and recording. Patricia Anderson came into the recording project as editor and director and offered clear and direct guidance.

Thanks to friends and colleagues who read and commented on the manuscript: Nick Alicino, Patricia Anderson, David Appelbaum, Barbara Bash, Leslie English, Steve Gorn, Jan Greenberg, Susan Grossman, Lanny Harrison, Jeff Moran, Andra Samelson, and Leland Williams.

Finally, my thanks to Susan Quasha, Charles Stein, and George Quasha of Station Hill Press, who offered skills, kindness, and support to bring this project to fruition.

Stephen Clorfeine

Accord, New York
August, 2000

To my parents, Myrtle Shemin Clorfeine and Solomon Clorfeine,
who took me on the road as soon as I could walk

and to my root Buddhist teacher, Chogyam Trungpa Rinpoche,
who pointed out another kind of journey

Map of Nepal and Her Neighbors

1

KATHMANDU JOURNAL

In Autumn 1995 I spent four months in Kathmandu as co-director of The Naropa University Study Abroad Program. It was my first journey to Asia and, though I've traveled all my life and lived abroad, nothing prepared me for Nepal.

It was another kind of wisdom, the tradition of Tibetan Buddhist meditation practice, that best informed my way. Kathmandu is a crazy place from a New York point of view, but instructive from a Buddhist one, where the slowed down, unpredictable texture of life begins to make sense. I hesitated at first and then settled into this texture.

I arrive on a Monday or Tuesday in early September, three days from New York's Hudson Valley—Newark, Los Angeles, Seoul, Bangkok, a few days, a few nights, I no longer know. In Boudnath, the Tibetan neighborhood of Kathmandu, it doesn't matter. Here it's Guru Rinpoche day.

Guru Rinpoche, Padmasambhava, eighth century saint of Northern India, now the number one Buddhist "deity" in the Kathmandu Valley. Legendary emanation of Buddha, born full grown on a lotus flower. Himalayan traveler retrieving hidden teachings of the Buddha Shakyamuni. His twenty-five disciples spawned all the Buddhist lineages, his hand and footprints mark meditation caves throughout the region, and his story is told in ceremonial dances high in Himalayan monasteries.

Our lodgings are steps away from the Great Stupa of Dharmakaya, a landmark of Boudnath, one of the most sacred Buddhist sites on the sub-continent, a one hundred foot tall concrete monument, representing the Buddha's enlightened body, speech and mind. Here, the early evening circumambulating has begun, the whole neighborhood pouring out, prayer beads and prayer wheels in hand.

On this first evening we're sitting in the Land of Snows restaurant, high above the crowds. I watch them stepping, strolling, prostrating in slow motion full body swoop onto the stone walkway around the Stupa. The sky changes color. Clouds darken, a steady stream of monks, nuns, and lay people chant mantras and light butter lamps. I watch the reflections of hundreds of tiny flames like waves of longing—and inside the restaurant the sound system pumps out Stevie Wonder, "I Just Called To Say I Love You."

September 6

I sit on the steps at the entrance to a local monastery and admire birds and trees. I see a small white cattle heron; a variety of rhododendron tree with one huge white flower; a black and white striped butterfly. These first days in Asia, deluged by the unfamiliar, it's a lot to take in. I'm absorbing sound, texture, scent, body language, while remaining in the background. Relieved to be part of the background, I start to get the hang of it. I like the pace.

There are reports that the nine month old Communist government is wavering, that soldiers are marching downtown, near the King's palace. We were going downtown, but now we decide to stay put here in Boudha, our neighborhood, twenty minutes away.

The next day we do go downtown. It's like going from Long Island City where I grew up, to Manhattan, except there are no traffic lights. The taxi dodges cows in repose, or ambling, munching, nursing, defecating. Our driver tries to pass everything on the road and other drivers do the same. Car horns announce every maneuver and there is constant blaring, joined by all, in both directions. Only bicyclists are silent, forced to the side or off the road. Pedestrians too are silent. Is this a cultural imperative, I wonder, to accept inequity?

In an appliance store my friend gives a rupee to a dazzling girlchild carrying a baby on her hip. Minutes later her mother, now carrying the baby, enters the shop and thrusts herself in front of me. I am startled and angry. What does she want? She pushes her open palm at my chest. I move away. She moves towards me. I move again. She moves with me. I cut an angle and she corners me. Now I feel threatened. What is going on here?

Just then the shop owner reaches between the woman and me and with sharp words, he stiffs her out the door. But when he moves to the back of the store, the woman returns and the whole thing is repeated. Later, I will be told by Nepalese friends how difficult it is to reverse the cycle of child beggars. Today I vow never to give money to children. Ever. I will repeat this vow over and over again, day in and day out.

Later in the afternoon I watch soldiers in camouflage, with bayonets and rifles, jump out of trucks and dash into formation on the Durbar Marg boulevard. Something is definitely happening. I remember the special travelers' evacuation insurance I considered and did not purchase.

This evening I see a dead man on the street. Half an hour before, he was lying against a wall but still breathing. Now, a gray blanket covers his body, some rupee notes lying on top. Like the soldiers in camouflage earlier today, something has come and gone. I'm starting to learn what it's like here. We keep on walking.

September 8

This morning I'm up at six after a late night Sherpa community center party outside one of my windows. Microphones, bands, motorcycles—they set up all day and partied from late afternoon on. In my room, I was their captive audience. From the other window I see young monks drift into the yard in the early morning to pee or to brush their teeth. Later, at recess, they play marbles, and then soccer, bare-chested or tee-shirted, maroon robes flying.

This full moon morning the Stupa is arranged for ritual feast practices—*pujas*. Butter lamps everywhere, makeshift tents cordoned off for practitioners. At the end of these feasts, dozens of children come to beg for food offerings—rice and sweets.

By now, I'm a regular at the Stupa as I circumambulate, clicking my prayer beads with the others. Here, folks gossip as they spin prayer wheels and repeat mantras. Spitting as they walk. Boys and men gamble in tight circles of bodies while lines of women sell fresh bread. Wild dogs live in a world of their own, lie about, mount each other, growl, snarl, scratch, limp. A stray cow, dazed and determined, wanders the Stupa grounds. A goat, always in the same spot, tied to a post, madly arching and scratching its back with its horns. A con man in the crowd, eyeing the Westerners, ready with a story for some innocent ear.

And the children. Images and after-images, of children. All sizes, castes, pursuits, dispositions. I have one favorite at the Stupa. Actually two. The coffee boy serves tea and coffee

early in the morning, pulling hard on the handle of the milk
steamer, as high as he is. He slides around the counter to
serve customers, takes time out to look after his baby
brother. When the morning rush is over, he plays tag with a
friend outside the shop, pausing to sell cookies, to collect
money from customers. His name is Dilba Durai. The other
child I see only from time to time. He rides on the back of his
begging brother. He is a Mongoloid with foreshortened limbs
and a magnificent mouth curved into a permanent smile.

September 9

I change money on the black market, at the notorious Nirvana
Guest House. People say, "*Just go to Krishna at the Nirvana*," but
I'm nervous anyway. The last time I did something like this in
Morocco thirty years ago, I wound up in a small tea shop in
the Kasbah late at night with a man I didn't know ordering tea
for me. When he stood up to greet a friend, I switched tea
cups with him.

So by the time we're actually in the lobby of the Nirvana
Guest House waiting for Krishna, I'm pacing around, sitting
down, crossing my legs, uncrossing my legs, standing up
again, and when I look into the garden, I find myself analyzing

the motives of the guests. Once we're in the back office with Krishna it goes smoothly, and though he is quite relaxed, I'm on edge for the rest of the day.

Finally, mission accomplished, padded with wads of rupee bills concealed in money belts and waist packs, I climb into a bicycle rickshaw. Images of nineteenth century Western imperialists arise but immediately give way to a fearful thrill like Coney Island's Steeplechase. We veer through crowds and traffic towards the Him Thai restaurant uphill on Lazimpat in the embassy section of town. To get there you cross an intersection—the only actual traffic light in Kathmandu. On a raised concrete dais in the center stands a white-uniformed, white-helmeted, white-gloved policeman waving his baton at traffic coming and going in four directions. It works. Thus conducted, traffic stops and starts on the green and red signals.

I wonder about the condition of the policeman's lungs, his heart, his eyes as Kathmandu is the second most polluted city in the world. Though many people cover their mouth and nose with cloth or gauze, I can't imagine this indomitable, Anglicized figure in a face mask.

Past the intersection, Lazimpat begins its climb through wide lanes with densely shaded rows of eucalyptus trees on either side. Spanish moss hangs from the branches, camouflage

21

for thousands of sleeping fruit bats. Later, I will come here to see and hear the rush of bat wings in the dusk.

September 10

How to describe Pashupatinath, the sacred Hindu complex sprawling with centuries of shrines where pilgrims come to die and cremation fires are always burning. It's a thirty minute walk from Boudnath along a deep rutted dirt road skirted by rice fields and lined with tin roofed huts of every description. People do so much of their living outdoors, in front of their huts: bathing, shaving, milling, drying and sorting grain, sewing on machines, preparing food, massaging babies.

This same dirt road is also a traffic route. Buses, trucks and livestock, lurch along, in and out of broad puddles. One quickly leaves the Tibetan area around the Stupa. Gradually, closer to the river, new houses appear with satellite dishes and elaborate balconies and brickwork.

Ancient and present wealth of bricks. Ubiquitous bricks, Nepal's secret: firing bricks, laying bricks, cleaning bricks, picking bricks, sorting bricks, piling bricks into stacks, tossing bricks into baskets on someone's back, placing bricks in your own basket on your own back.

We cross a river, a tributary of the Bagmati; climb a hundred stone steps and reach a park of Hindu shrines, dozens and dozens of small and large monuments to Shiva, in his pleasant form of Pashupati, protector of animals. As I walk the gauntlet between walls crowded with monkeys, any one of them ready to leap at the slightest provocation, I feel completely unprotected.

Hindu gods have so many manifestations and their interrelationships are a complex web, a family network whose elaboration has provided employment for centuries of scholars. Shiva, part of the trinity with Brahma and Vishnu, has a multitude of emanations, ranging from the dancing, wife-embracing teacher to dark, fierce Bhairav in sixty-four terrifying forms.

Shiva is the most powerful. He's the god of ascetics. These Hindu holy men, *sadhus*, heads covered with ashes, foreheads with symbolic painted lines, carry tridents as staffs and hold begging bowls. Around Pashupati, their authenticity varies. Showmen, some of them, dressed to the nines in wild face paint and wrapped in colorful lengths of cotton. Other *sadhus* one observes in complete stillness, their eyes peaceful, radiant.

Looking down from above the towering Golden Temple, the sprawling hospices, hotels and nursing homes define the residential center of Pashupati. It's an inner city of holiness on the west side of the river, arrayed with all the daily activity that Hindus perform. While boys swim naked and cows wade and drink, Brahmin men go about their daily ablutions. While families wait nearby, cremation pyres are stacked with wood and cloth-wrapped bodies are placed on top. The amount of wood, the height of the pyre, is determined by caste or wealth.

Vendors sell everything from incense to bangles to buddhas. They surround you, stop you in your tracks, come at you from all sides. Anything goes. Women, children, and men practice an alternation of charm and first degree aggression. When their tactics become outrageous, I burst out laughing, and murmur phrases that they don't understand but make me feel better: *"You gotta be kidding me. I can buy that cheaper on 14th Street." "I'll take a hundred of those. Can you pack them and send them with my driver?"*

At one point a wild *sadhu*, dreadlocks wound high on top of his head, tall iron trident in hand, misunderstands what I've shouted ahead to my companion. He shakes the trident in the air and screams like he's threatening to kill me. For a moment I feel trapped, and though he's standing twenty feet away, I remain frozen. Am I tourist prey or is this holy warfare?

September 12

My first walk alone. I climb through Asan, the major shopping district of Kathmandu. By the time I get to the top, my senses are exhausted. At Indrchowk, the textile district, I walk past every shop and stall and take a casual inventory.

I turn down a side street and begin to wander. Aware that I've abandoned the route I've carefully studied on the map, I pretend to pay attention to the twists and turns, the direction of the sun, the time. But soon I'm lost in another kind of walking where I no longer look at things, yet still absorb what I pass through or what passes through me. I *want* to be lost. I walk like one possessed. I am possessed. The mood of daily life. The neighborhood. It's a familiar and reckless state of tourist delight.

I think about consulting the map. I think about calculating time and distance, but the sun dips over the water and a strong evening light takes over. As dusk approaches, I climb out of the city along a hillside of shacks and gardens. At every turn I look back, but I can no longer locate the horizon. I swing back to the road, the children at play around me, the gardens and the garbage. The sun has set and I must return.

Tomorrow the students arrive. I have responsibilities for which I'm being paid.

I'm looking to orient myself. The next signpost I see is Tribuvan University. I enlist a group of students to help me find my way back to town. First they smile, then laugh, then discuss things among themselves, then look at me with an equal measure of shyness and audacity. Finally, they piece together a question in English that essentially repeats what I have just asked them.

From there, it all goes sideways. We never really progress into an answer or even a confirmation. Instead, we amble downhill in a shifting formation with all of them on various sides of me full steam into a minor interrogation. *"Where are you from? What are you doing? Do you like Nepal? America is very good. You have lot of money. Nepal is poor country."*

For a while I parry with questions of my own. *"What do you study? What classes are you in? Where do you live?"* But as it grows darker I am anxious to find my way. So far there's been no agreement among them on how I get back to Durbar Marg. Every time I bring it up, there's a volley of opinions, pointed fingers, laughter and private commentary. With a strategy that will later be second nature to me in Nepal, I zero in on one student and address all my questions to him. In the end, it is

26

determined that the best idea is to get into an auto rickshaw. But then the bargaining ceremonies begin and they are lousy at it. They don't use taxis and so they carry on like we're in a sitcom until I just get in and name my price. At that moment, the student I've singled out, jumps in beside me. It's beyond me to figure out what will happen now, and after a half-hearted attempt to ask him if perhaps he lives in this direction, we settle in for the ride.

He is delighted. In this two seat, three wheel vehicle, he has me all to himself. I'm wedged between the cardboard thin door and him; between amusement and anxiety. I suspect the worst—that he'll ask for money or try to sell me drugs. But as we approach Durbar Marg, he pulls a wallet from his pocket and hands me a small identity photo—of himself. Just as I realize he means for me to keep it, he looks solemnly into my eyes and says, "*Never forget me.*"

I slowly raise my gaze in astonishment as I try to register what I'm getting into here. He carefully withdraws the photo and writes his name on the back: *Rajendra Kumar*. Again, he hands it back to me. "*Never forget me,*" he repeats. As the rickshaw stops, I pat his shoulder and shake his hand. Walking away, I feel his dark eyes follow me down the street. I resist the urge to turn and wave.

For the next three months the photo lies in my desk drawer, the object, which I can't seem to discard, now more haunting than the experience. After several months and many encounters with young Nepalese men, I piece together the substance of this dramatic behavior. For those who have had some higher education or contact with Westerners, the horizon of their native lives seems forever dim. In Nepal, they will never earn a salary that will provide opportunities. Only through contact with foreigners, by attracting a benefactor, will they find the money or situation to alter their path from what feels like a dead end. It's heartbreaking to me when I finally recognize this.

From time to time I pick up the tiny identity photo and hear his voice, *"Never forget me."* Rajendra Kumar.

September 16

I am introduced to Chime, a Tibetan street lady known to all at the Great Stupa, where she's been living for years in varying degrees of health. The story told me is that when she was a university student, extremely bright and devoted, she went off the deep end and never returned. For Chime, life in the deep end is an alternation of delight and agony. Not so different from the rest of us.

Another part of her story is that a year ago a famous Tibetan teacher saw her and made her a nun on the spot. So sometimes Chime wears nun's robes and I call her Chime Rinpoche. When she's feeling good, she's up for anything. When she's down, she only wants money.

Chime carries bags with her all the time. Plastic store bags and a new day pack. The day pack complements an outfit of tight black jeans, nylon windbreaker and high heeled sneakers. It all makes sense when you've seen her work the tourist crowd in a wonderful broken English. You never know what she will say. Sometimes, she reads your thoughts. Trailing behind me, with a bouncing walk and grunting laughter, she tosses flowers at passersby. Flowers she has stolen from all the shrines.

One day she's a butterfly. "I'm Butterfly," she shrieks. It's infectious. I laugh and feel instantly lightheaded. Her madness is liberating. "I'm Butterfly. I have flower. I'm Butterfly. I have flower." When she opens her sketchbook, we turn the pages together, while a crowd gathers. Most are amused, friendly, but some make fun of her, and worse, she is sometimes robbed and beaten. At those times she's morose, helpless. But a few days later, she appears in a silk *chuba*, relatively clean and smiling.

We are instant friends but the depth of it surprises me. I take her to tea and insist when the waiter tries to get rid of her. Every time I think I'm doing good, I'm faced with a whining madwoman who wants something. If I try ignoring her, it's at once evident that facing her is simpler.

Then there are circumstances when she just pops up and catches me by surprise. I jump back and turn around to find her tickling my neck with a feather. *"Chime you're a spider."* "I *spider.*" She roars with child energy: "I *spider.*"

Friends from New York join us for tea. I introduce Chime and she sits quietly, almost demure. I wonder if she recalls another lifetime or the time before she flipped. I can't deny the thought that she might be a *tulku*, a teacher re-born. In Tibetan folklore, some teachers manifest as madwomen. The Buddhist saint Naropa's first yearning for a guru is instigated by an outrageous crone, a cleaning woman who taunts him and challenges his certainty that he understands the sacred texts. When he begs her to help him find a master, he is initiated into his search for self-realization.

My favorite Chime drawing is a circle with an infinity sign inside it, surrounded by flowers with faces on either side. When we turn the page to it, Chime announces: "*Man, woman, world, samsara.*" Represented by the infinity sign, *samsara* is the endless turning alternation of pain and pleasure. "*Man, woman, world, samsara.*" I am pondering this when Chime tears off the sheet and hands it to me. "*This one for you.*" Then she says, "*Your father is looking for you.*" Tears come to my eyes. He died ten years ago but at this moment, I feel like I could turn around and see him.

September 19

It's been raining for two days, the only part of true monsoon weather we've encountered. And though we've gotten off easy, still, it's odd without the sun. Then one morning I see white peaks from my window. Just at dawn their light beckons me awake. I rush to the roof of the guest house. There they are— Himalayan peaks dazzling in a pink blanket of sky.

September 23

Makunda-gi. Makunda Raj Ariel, native anthropologist/historian, orthodox Brahmin, de-coder of the secrets of Hinduism. He leads us through magnificent ancient Bhaktipur, once a powerful city-state, the location of extraordinary wooden carved architectural facades and seventeenth century windows, casually hanging among slums, next to large advertising signs for Coca-Cola, along a continuous trail of dead rats, and small kids defecating off the curb, where there is a curb.

Surrounding the city there are still some rice fields, but throughout the Kathmandu Valley new construction—houses, roads, carpet factories—has sprawled over the rice paddy countryside of twenty years ago.

Makunda-gi delivers a three hour lecture covering the history of Nepal from pre-history to present. His teeth and palate are at odds with each other, his fingernails bitten, and at any break in the action he glues a cigarette to his lower lip. In syncopated British sing-song, Makunda-gi lectures us:

"Can you imagine a country with thirty-six distinct geological divisions and only eighteen million people? Can you imagine? Yet up to this time there has been no reliable archeological excavation in the

Kathmandu Valley. There are no stones or tools or signs of pre-historic age. Even stone tools found to the south do not match any local quarry, suggesting they must have been smuggled in from Tibet. My friends, I hold up these facts for your discernment. I have been working in the field for thirty-five years, long before Western museum people arrived in Nepal."

About Western museum people he has little good to say.

Makunda-gi is a politician at large, whose intelligence and shrewdness are belied by his careless exterior. He assesses the current regime with the passion of an armchair general. Out on the street, he dangles babies in the crook of his arm and receives their slobber on his face, cigarette intact. He shoos beggars away when their come-on is too demanding for us, and for our benefit, he uses people as exhibits. Grabbing the ear of a squatting old man Makunda-gi declaims:

"You see his earring? That is a special sign that this man has received the gift bestowed on any person who has reached the age of seventy-seven years, seven months, seven weeks and seven days. When a person reaches the age of eighty-eight years, eight months, eight weeks and eight days, he receives a second earring. Can you imagine, he is driven around the village in a chariot. This is the way we honor old people in our society."

I want to ask about ninety-nine years, nine months, nine weeks, but in Nepal the average life-span is fifty-two years of age.

September 25

Kathmandu, the capital of this tiny Hindu monarchy of Nepal wedged between world giants China and India, holds a wealth of folklore. The origin myth of the Great Stupa of Dharmakaya links Nepal and Tibet through the Bodhisattva, Avalokiteshvara. Avalokiteshvara is divine compassion and the original Bodhisattva. He appears in billions of forms like falling rain for those ready to receive him. He brought Buddhism to Tibet where he tamed the regional barbarians and established Samye Ling, the first Tibetan monastery.

Avalokiteshshvara made a vow to his guru, the Buddha Amitabha, that he would liberate all sentient beings from the misery of this world. But looking out from the top of Tibet's Potala Palace in Lhasa, he saw so many creatures so miserable, that he realized his vow was impossible to achieve and he wept. From his teardrops were born to King Indra two daughters—Purna, whose name means complete, and Apurna, incomplete. Apurna, as punishment for stealing flowers, was

34

reborn in the human realm in Nepal to a poultryman and his wife. She was named Shamvara and she did so well as a poultrywoman, that she could establish her four sons as educated householders. She did so well that her only further wish was to honor her faith. And though she died before its completion, her four sons finished the task of building the Great Stupa of Dharmakaya. In turn each of them was granted a wish for rebirth and each chose a life as a royal protector of Buddhism in Tibet.

October 1

Mornings are different now. Clouds of fog sit over the valley until eight or nine o'clock and bring damp chill to waking and to morning meditation. But days are still hot—eighty degrees—and often humid.

Deep pollution and dust make an ordinary head cold feel like penance. My buttons are pushed. In a morning dream, I come across a small branch full of birds I've never seen. Suddenly, excited, I recognize them as turtle doves. *"You see,"* I say to my companion, *"they have turtle shells on their backs."* At that moment they flap and fly off, shrieking, hundreds and hundreds of them.

Just yesterday, the Buddhist master, Chokyi Nyima Rinpoche, held a marigold in his hand and said, *"If we call it a flower it is not true. If we feel its essence, that is closer."*

I remember a favorite story, *"Funes Memorius,"* by the Argentine writer Borges, where Funes, the genius boy, lies paralyzed for years. Frustrated by the imprecision of language, he invents words to describe each leaf, each time of day, each kind of light. Thousands of new words for each moment to moment witnessing. Words without a history. Words without anything but essence.

October 3

Today is the anniversary of His Holiness Khyentse Rinpoche's death or *paranirvana*. One of the most revered teachers of this century, I'd met him several times in North America and received his teachings. The display of butter lamps at the Great Stupa is monumental. Sechen, his monastery, is strung on all sides, top to bottom with thousands of tiny white Christmas lights. Candles line the monks' quarters and everywhere monks of all ages are lighting and re-lighting them. We join in, light candles, speak the names of sick and dying friends. This is a Tibetan holiday. Celebrating the death of a great teacher, *mahasiddha*, great enlightened one.

On the way back, we follow the sound of singing to Thrangu Rinpoche's monastery, climb the steps, and stand at the door to a large bare room where two dozen young monks practice their evening lessons. The little ones alternate singing and reciting, their voices fully embodied.

My heart opens so easily here—opens and opens—so delicately that the slightest shift leaves its mark, like tonight, when a boisterous little monk uses his whole body to belt his voice out in a cracking pitch.

The next day, I show some students a photograph of Khentse Rinpoche. Radiant, beaming. Six and a half feet tall, bare chest, white pony tail. Mr. Universe.

October 5

I've lived here now for one month and I find myself in full conversation with the place: a rubber tree with myriad tendrils loose like Medusa's hair; stark evergreens, in formation like dance partners, next to flowering tropical trees; wooden masks with skeleton faces—wrathful protectors—inside a dark

and crammed antique shop off the bright boulevard; boys
games with marbles—in the dirt, on the street, in the fields;
black and tan crows perched on our rooftop clothes line,
slowly chewing through the rope as they sit there; the way
dogs go through garbage (and goats, cows, street kids go
through garbage); scenes through doorways into courtyards,
through alleyways into fields, across fields to monasteries; the
smile on the face of a beggar boy when he's given an entire
bag of rice and sweets.

I've been here for a month now and I see things differently, my mind works differently. You can't take anything for
granted. My list of things to do: buy everything in sight for
best possible price; write long letters to all friends; stabilize
mind and accumulate awareness until continuous awareness
arises, then liberate all beings from *samsara*. In the meantime
pay restaurant bill, make phone call, prepare for class.

October 11

From my perch above the Stupa this morning I can see
trekking season moving into full swing, video cameras and
mountain gear everywhere. A confluence of movements:
trekkers to the Himalayan peaks; Hindus with blood sacrifices

to thirsty Kali shrines; and in my Western daybook it's Yom Kippur, the holiest of Jewish days, when Jews fast to atone for their sins.

Bouncing and winding in a taxi up the foothills to Parphing, I'd like to imagine the driver enjoys this excursion into cleaner air but getting out of the city is a trip in itself. It's the last shopping day before the great Hindu holiday, Dessain, a ten day celebration of *Shakti*, the mother goddess, and the streets are packed with markets and buyers. It's like Manhattan—if you live in the middle, you drive through a lot of city to get out.

Parphing. A village flush with autumn crops, flowers, dirty children, all beckoning like the hills we'll climb to Parphing monastery, to the famous Guru Rinpoche cave on top.

There are kites everywhere. This is high season when boys dedicate themselves to getting kites aloft. Little ones run with mock kites—bits of plastic on a string. All Nepalese know about kites and the pros can show you how to attach slivers of metal for kite battles. Our guest house roof is filled with battle cries, wounded kites and shouts of help for tangled kite string lines.

Two boys lead the way up the Parphing hills. One is quiet, the other manic, keeps a broken wheel rolling by poking it with a stick. You see boys play at this all the time with wheels from the size of a fist to car tires. Today the wheel boy runs along, prodding an old bike wheel, shouting scraps of English phrases. His eyes are wild and he whips the wheel violently until just at the top of the first hill it falls apart, collapses. Then he quiets down.

Halfway up, our group of four stops at a Nyingma monastery, where young monks, squatting on patio stones, practice scribing Tibetan alphabet letters on slates. An old monk, one of their teachers, works a scissors through another monk's hair, smiling broadly then laughing a great belly laugh when I photograph them.

A final steep climb brings us to the monastery that surrounds the Guru Rinpoche cave. Inside the cave we light candles, sit cross-legged on our backpacks and chant the *Sadhana of Mahamudra*, written by my root teacher, Chogyam Trungpa Rinpoche. Words translated from an old Tibetan text resonate in the cave: *"Good, bad, happy, sad, all thoughts vanish like the imprint of a bird in the sky."*

On the way down when we stop at Dakshenkali, a temple compound where weekly animal sacrifices are made, we move deep into Hindu ritual. A continuous line of sacrifices has been made today and pools of watery blood are everywhere, running in rivulets as boys hose down the stone floors. People wait in line with their animals, and in order we watch them beheaded: a rooster, a duck, a chicken, a small goat. Each animal unceremoniously handed to the executioner, whose knife is deft. The head is returned to the owner while blood from the severed body is squirted onto small Kali statues. Kali, consort of Shiva, is the goddess of time or death, divine representative of the destructive aspect of cosmic energy. The animal's twitching body is laid on the ground until lifted by the owner and carried away by its legs.

Drink Kali. Drunken blood of barnyard beasts. Drink Kali, wife of Shiva. Empower yourself to slay the troublesome demons. Terrify non-believers. With your wrathful countenance, wake us up.

October 14

I hike with a friend to Pullihari Monastery, the seat of His Eminence Jamgon Kongtrul Rinpoche, a wonderful young Tibetan teacher killed in a car accident in 1991. I knew him over a period of fifteen years and he was kind to me on many occasions. Pullihari means hill of flowers and is named after the monastery where Naropa gave final teachings to his disciple, Marpa the Translator, who then carried Buddhism to Tibet.

Muggy day, overcast and still, dust kicks up easily and every passing vehicle raises clouds of it. It settles back down on everything including my open video camera. Along the way locals smile easily and show off babies. Children literally jump and prance in front of me. Everyone laughs when I aim the camera at goats, pigs and chickens.

I think I've never met gentler people, soft and gracious in their own way. Children, from toddlers up, on their own so much of the time, their own lives, their own adventures.

Pullihari, hill of flowers, with its sweeping view of the valley and surrounding hills and valleys. Spacious, terraced stone walks. Plantings of lilies, roses, bougainvillea, fields of tall perennial marigolds, arbors and vegetable gardens. At dusk, with monks chanting, horns and drums clattering. Then stillness. Monastery life—time suspended.

On the walk down, a group of four boys attaches itself to us. It's clear that they will accompany us until we send them back. Of course they want their pictures taken. I hold them off for a while until I remember a beautiful banyan tree on a rock ledge further down and tell them I'll film them under the tree. When we get there, they scramble eagerly into formation. With giggles they attempt a song but lacking most of the lyrics, it subsides until the tallest of them, a boy named Anil, offers to perform a dance. He begins to move forward and back. His entire bearing changes as he solemnly skips and sings, his eyes flashing:

"Today I cut grass. I bring the clippings to my mother and father and they feed them to the animals. Some we use to make beds for the cows."

I work with him on his English. I worry that I prompt him too much. Why do I need an explanation? Whose words do I want to hear? Will anyone else notice that Anil is a jewel? I want him to have a world where his intelligence will flourish, where his spirit will make a difference.

October 15

A German friend tells me that a Tibetan teacher advised him to think of the Buddha first thing in the morning upon waking, and to mix that with thoughts of the day ahead. When I wake up, I'm so determined about the schedule that I go about the program with a vengeance. Then the pace of life here, so unpredictable, dissolves the schedule as the day progresses. This dispersion also is buddha activity.

When I bring the laundry to Snow White Dry Cleaners, I wait while each piece is sorted, each name and color translated and written down. The young man's slow careful movements give me time to practice patience, compassion. My mind doesn't wander. It takes months to remember that slow is not dull—it is repetition—contact with the same act over and over.

October 17

Time is passing. In two weeks we have a break in the semester. Another staff member and I are planning a trek in the Annapurna region of the Himalayas. We've been reading and re-reading guidebooks and comparing notes. Should we take the Western slope or Eastern slope? Cross the seventeen thousand foot pass or linger and wander along the way? Time is passing and now I'm accustomed to the impossible.

Here in Nepal you wouldn't say, *"Please don't shake your dustpan out on the sidewalk;" "Don't spit brown and yellow gobs of mucous and tobacco juice at my feet;" "Don't pour dirty water out your window while I'm passing by."*

Here in Nepal, you mind your step, eyes alert to all phenomena. Glance at open meat stalls, at animal heads, guts, intestines. Or not. Inhale open sewage. Or not. Cover your mouth and nose. Or not.

My lungs full of dust and fumes—I cough and spit like they do. Walk through garbage, breathe face to face with beggars, brush against maimed bodies, squeeze into small buses with too many others. Like they do. My daily acquaintances are a friendly con man, a displaced monk, a tiny laughing waiter. Don't speculate on who you've become. Here, it works.

Mind like garden practice, on knees like prayer, wrists curled, trowel in hand, probe the earth. Worm, beetle, onion grass, smooth tomato, prickly cucumber, whatever comes up. Apple baked with cardamom, Darjeeling tea with cardamom, teeth yellow with cardamom, whatever comes up. Stupa bells, Tibetan horns, squeaky prayer wheels, whatever comes up.

My life as I knew it, things I did, responsibilities I had, are so far away. I want to wander, absorb the quality of things, the pleasure of daily, random encounters. Ongoing sense of emptiness. Not resisting it. What is simple—is simple.

October 20

Things about Nepal: women, bent over small brooms made of grasses; moments later the dust returns—daily layers of dust; people urinating anywhere—throwing food and paper scraps into the street. Washing in the street: at spigots, fountains, with hoses, buckets—face, hair, teeth, body—men wash in underwear or bathing suits, women wash in saris, sometimes topless. Children on bicycles—little ones ride the handle bars; whole families on scooters—women ride sidesaddle, ankles crossed, saris and shawls flying.

What people carry through the streets: sofas, bales of hay, sheaves of rice, piles of tin trunks, dining room tables, stacks of chairs, oil in plastic containers, grains, fruits, yogurt, milk buckets. And on their bicycles, wheeling along like moveable shops—one hand balances the load.

Vehicle etiquette for squeezing by on small roads: endless shouts and hand signals; buses and trucks always carry a boy who jumps out to expedite maneuvers. Thick black diesel exhaust of tractors, dump trucks, buses, three wheeled rickshaws—steady plumes of black smoke.

Road repair: one man or woman shovels gravel into pans held by others. The pan loads are tossed into the street. This is repeated. Don't stop for traffic, just shift your weight, twist your torso, move the sand. Move the sand, one pile to another. Everyday. One pile to another. Everyday.

October 21

In the evening, before dusk, I walk to the river and sit at the base of a holy footprint, next to a shrine of Bhairav, protector deity, one of the sixty-four wrathful images of Shiva. Many armed Bhairav, naked, black, with a necklace of human skulls and mighty weapons. Today it's Tihar, a five day Hindu festival celebrating the victory of light over darkness, of aspiration for enlightenment over ignorance of self-realization. The shrines are richly praised and Bhairav is drenched in buttery red cinnabar paste.

I watch a river snake, a goldfinch, another small bird with a rust colored tail. Behind me, Shiva's bull Nandi, and the omnipresent lingam/yoni shapes in stone—symbols of procreation, reproduction. Behind Bhairav, a tethered cow and a sleeping dog. Across this narrow stretch of river a Ganesh monument bathed and spread with orange *tikka* paste. The beautiful elephant headed son of Shiva, Ganesh.

Bhairav hovers over me. The slight movement of his shadow causes me to turn as though someone had spoken to me. This is the protection of the deity.

October 24

Today I return to Nagi Gompa, the nunnery where Tulku Urgyen Rinpoche resides. This time 250 people ascend the mountain for his annual public seminar. Tulku Urgyen is one of the last great old Tibetan teachers in the Kathmandu Valley. Every Tibetan knows of his residence at Nagi Gompa, and knows of his accomplishments.

Tulku Urgyen Rinpoche is one of the reasons I took this job. I know little about him, but what I know has shifted the way I see my life. He speaks about the accumulation of moments of awareness as a gradual path to approach enlightenment. And when I met him here three weeks ago, everything about those twenty-four hours felt auspicious, each step resonant in coincidence, in meaning—the teachings at work.

"Look, look at your own mind. Mind itself does not exist anywhere. This non-existent mind is the great wonder of the variety of appearance. Mind is merely appearance. That mind of all sentient beings is the wisdom of great bliss, incomprehensible, complete nonthought, appearing as the nature of luminosity."

In the large shrine room the walls are covered by paintings of emanations of Buddhas. In the corners, ten foot high statues of Avalokiteshvara, the Buddha of Compassion, and Tara, consort of the Buddha of Perfection and the Buddha of Boundless Success. Last time I slept under the Tara and dreamed about a beautiful young woman who became my wife. Tonight I will sleep under the Buddha of Compassion, surrounded by warm butter lamps.

Now, as coolness folds into evening, I put my hood up, wrap my scarf, and sit at the edge of the hill thinking about stories of leopards. The ring of high mountains darkens—blue shadows settle over everything and the early twilight is suddenly luminous. Lines and lines of prayer flags connect heaven, earth, and the night itself. I wonder, is there enough protection? Then in the still air, a breeze comes up and all the prayer flags flap at once, hundreds and hundreds of them.

October 28

These days the fog lifts early. By seven the sky is clear and every morning I gaze at snow peaks in the distance. We're all counting the days until the break. My trekking partner and I hold daily logistics discussions. The atmosphere at the guest house is saturated with the promise of adventure.

How quickly one gets used to things. How quickly one hardly notices. As I watch a woman pull a comb through her dark wet hair, I remember how unusual it seemed at first, this grooming on the street—women combing each other's hair, searching out lice; men holding hands, lying in each other's laps. How comforting these easy going, physical gestures, so close to earth, to animals. There is such pleasure in the gentleness of it. I want to move, touch, and be touched with that gentleness.

Here in Kathmandu, the valley of the gods, I've come to understand a truth that isn't easily expressed. Protection lies in acceptance, in openness—the light touch of surrender.

Map of Annapurna

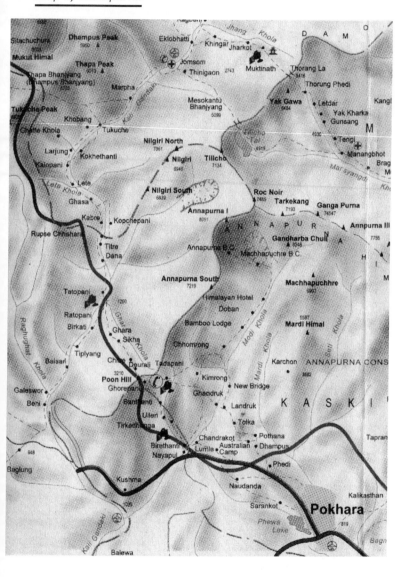

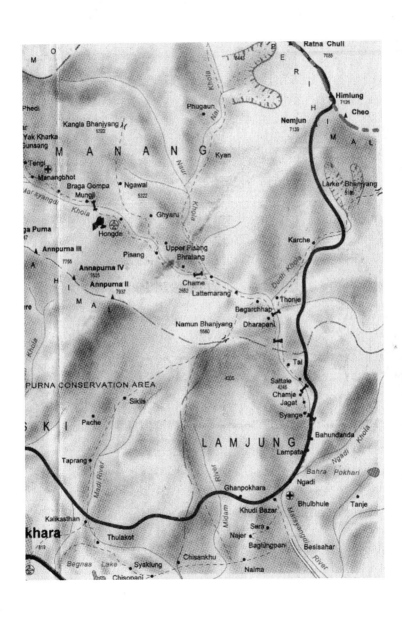

2

ANNAPURNA—
DOWN THE WESTERN SLOPE

I'd been living in Nepal for two months now and I'd absorbed some of the spirit and mechanics of the culture. Trekking is part of that culture, but has its own paradigm. One considers altitude, climate, attire, lodging, and health in a very different way from our ordinary lives: survival overshadows comfort. In fact, as soon as one takes a hard look at the Himalayas, comfort disappears from view altogether.

At the moment of landing on the airstrip, nine thousand feet above sea level, I knew my perceptions were being altered in a way that would imprint my imagination for a long time. It was like meeting a landscape from another lifetime, immediately recognizing its essence, yet feeling giddy, uncertain of its origin or location in one's past. Slowly and certainly, as my senses adjusted to the startling barrenness of high terrain, to daily dramatic shifts in the environment, to encounters and exchange with local people along the way, I came to feel more and more grounded, tuned in. The constancy of walking, the rawness and the changeability, burned away concepts and left me as open, as receptive as I've ever felt.

November 3

A few days before setting out for the Annapurna range, I talked with a naturalist in Kathmandu. He showed me with delicate movements of his hands how the Himalayas were formed: the pressure of two continents clashing, pushing the land mass of one upward into peaks. The fingers of one hand held vertical are the peaks, and spread apart, I imagine glaciers and valleys in the empty gaps between his fingers.

Now I'm flying west to Pokhara, a resort town on Phewa Lake, the starting point for treks in the Annapurna region. Slow, suspended, the small plane moves gently across the valley. Soon I see luminous snow peaks—a massive range stretching above the hills. This is the outermost mandala.

Within the hills, patterns of terraced farmland appear like geographic contour maps. Brown rice fields, green grasses, then a deep dry gorge, then a wider gorge weaving through hills of barren red earth and isolated farmsteads. Further west, whitewater river gorges.

Twenty-five minutes into the flight the propellers cut back and we hover above cultivated valleys, above evergreen forests where white rapids cut through sandy banks. We descend across gorge after gorge. Then black sheep, white sheep, turquoise rivers and palm trees, lush gardens, green rice fields—the landing strip. The plane's wheels groan, shudder and labor into position.

In the town of Pokhara, I shop for expedition gear, rent sleeping bags, and hire porters. Eating lunch in the late afternoon, I read Jeremy Bernstein's Himalayan account in the New Yorker. He writes, *"There seems to be a genuine sense of well-being among people on all levels of the economic scale...I have come away with the feeling that I had been among a population of reasonably happy and often joyous people."*

November 4

Kagbeni at 10,500 feet. Up the western slope to Jomsom, the district seat of Lower Mustang, then a three hour walk along the Kali Gandaki river bed and up a rocky incline to this fortified medieval town. I am transported to a place I've never dreamed of, a world glimpsed only in photographs of mountaineers and nomads. I'm so dazzled, I nearly forget the sleepless night just past—the dysentery cramps, the dogs barking, bats swarming, water running, doors creaking, mosquitoes, other trekkers banging around and whispering loudly at four A.M.

57

The impressions of this first day are so intense: the flight to Jomson on an old Russian Aeroflot helicopter; disembarking into a cold fifty mile an hour gale; eating oat porridge with apples in a lodge close to the airstrip where an Austrian trekking party packs and re-packs food supplies and expatriate Americans talk about their jobs in Singapore; outside, on the trail, the changing light and temperature; stripping layer after layer down to a tee-shirt; wending over small boulders embedded in the river bottom; the first ascent of cliffs; seeing farmers planting, maneuvering animals and plows, their singing, whistling, shouting; donkey trains and goatherds, yaks, moving up and down the trails.

At night, eating supper at the New Kali Gandaki Lodge, sitting on long benches with our feet under a table covered by heavy wool blankets. Under the blankets, the eldest daughter places buckets of wood charcoal which warm our feet and legs.

I stare, transfixed, at the supply cupboard—at hand stitched wool gloves, hats, miniature thangka paintings, plastic bags of short macaroni, a wheel of yak cheese, one chunk missing, cups, saucers, tall glasses, paper containers of *Fraati* apple drink, picture postcards, greetings from Denver, London, Hong Kong, potato chips, candy, crackers, toilet paper,

Snickers, decks of cards, cigarette lighters, half pints of vodka, rum, brandy. The glass doors are shut with small padlocks.

At eight P.M. I'm inside my sleeping bag under layers and layers of clothes, and more heavy blankets.

November 5

The town of Kagbeni is over six hundred years old. Today, at 6:30 in the morning, the town is quiet. Stretched out in my sleeping bag, gazing through the ground floor window that faces onto the street, I watch women move about with animals. Other women carry baskets on their backs, woven splint cylinders strapped with leather around their foreheads. This is how people carry goods up and down the mountain trails, and some of the older porters have deep permanent indentations on their brow.

The fortified section of the town is a labyrinth of tall, mud-walled buildings, corrals, storehouses, human dwellings, distinguishable one from another only by who or what is inside. The doorways and entrances to houses are protected by animal skulls and horns, tridents, wooden and stone carvings. Tunneled walkways lead to abandoned ruins of ancient forts and palaces elaborately built in stone and mud.

59

These are reminders of the power and prestige this place once held.

Kagbeni is the border of Lower and Upper Mustang. Local travelers and herders cross back and forth but the northern region, the ancient hidden Kingdom of Mustang, is semi-autonomous and still ruled by its own King. It is restricted to foreigners. I linger at the border station looking out across the great salt trade route, still used by gypsy traders. I imagine walking into the secret realm, giving a bribe—*baksheesh*—to buy a few hours in the real kingdom. When I test the limits and wander across the bridge, I am immediately called back by the border guards.

Inside the old town, children run wild, jump from stone ledges into a huge pile of straw and manure, climb back up and jump down again. I watch them and after five minutes they enlist me in their play, throwing themselves at me to be swung around and tossed in the air. Like all toddlers, they persist, *again*, *do it again*, no end in sight.

Even though I'm finished with the game, they continue to hurl their compact wool padded bodies against my legs. These children are fierce. They are also covered with a mixture of mucous, blood, and manure. The mucous is a by-product of the altitude. The manure is from the pile of straw. I don't know where the blood comes from. My hands, arms, clothes now streaked with all of this, I retreat to clean myself in the icy river water and avoid looking back.

Five yaks stand clustered together in a large stone and wood pen outside the New Kali Gandaki Lodge. They are large animals with long shaggy coats, a single hump, curved horns, and sweet, cow-like faces. Huge brown eyes. Starting mid-afternoon and continuing the next day and for days onwards, teams of men slaughter them one at a time. Then the skinning begins. Primitive tools are used: axe, knife, and mallet. In powerful movements, the men slam the mallet into the hind-quarters to loosen the hide, slide the knife in to cut the tissue, yank the hide away from the skin. Slam the mallet in again, until inch by inch, the hide is removed. Sometimes the blunt end of an axe is used on the opposite side of the heavy body to release hide from skin. Hooves, tail, ears, scrotum, are sawed off. Intestines are severed, and the blood is drained into pails.

These beasts are the economy of the plateau. Every part of the animal is used. People come from Kagbeni and sur-rounding villages to collect shares of meat, skin, bone, blood, organs. I notice a hierarchy about who gets what and when. You see people walking along the roads carrying a yak shank across their shoulders or smaller pieces in baskets on their backs. For the next week, we will pass people hauling yak parts across the plateau.

Walking back through the labyrinth, numbed by sun, wind, and slaughter, I watch a family load a pack of mules with bags of manure. A teenager works together with a young man hauling and lifting huge sacks, while a woman watches and smiles at us. It's impossible to know what age people are. They are small, children often years older than their size indicates, and adults age quickly up here on the plateau. Yet older people carry heavy loads and squat gracefully on their haunches.

Back at the Kali Gandaki Lodge, I play a game of mimicking faces with the five-year-old son of the lodge owner. His concentration is adept—he captures the emotion of each face. He too is caked in dirt, blood and mucous even though he lives in good surroundings. These are marks of their lives, not marks of measured poverty. The boy takes off his tee-shirt exposing three large wounds on the side of his chest.

I keep thinking about the yak slaughter. The killing and butchering is clean. What gets to me is the kids. They bounce on the back, play with the head, manipulate the tail of the yak's bloody body. Then they taunt the other yaks whose front legs are tied together, by throwing stones at them, making them jump and fall or stumble. Then the children laugh. Now I understand why their clothes are streaked with blood.

November 7

Looking for a day hike I notice a dot on the Mustang map with the name Pilling. My trekking partner, Lauren and I take the trail across the river from Kagbeni, and turn left along a steep ridge heading south down the river. Loosely cut by packs of animals, by farmers and traders, the trail changes in consistency from packed dirt, to loose shale, to sand, to dust. It's clear this trail is not used regularly. It's been washed out by rain, snow, and rockslides, so the ground literally shifts beneath our feet.

On our way to the bridge I glanced into the corral and noticed that another of the black and white yaks had been slaughtered. Now, we pass a man with a basket of yak meat. Soon after, large shadows appear. Across the river flocks of small black birds and delicate gray and white doves start up, as if frightened. And there, directly above us, massive vultures soar and glide, their shadows preceding them. I am stunned by their proximity. I had studied the pictures of the Lammergeirs, Steppe eagles and Egyptian vultures in my guidebook. These are the Himalayan griffon, with a five foot wingspan, short broad tail, and a white underbelly. Looking up at them, with nowhere to move away, I feel apprehensive. There are eight in all. I count and re-count them, trying to gain some equilibrium as they circle and swoop above our heads. Maybe it's some kind of omen—a warning about straying from the beaten path?

The outskirts of Pilling are stone fenced farm fields. We lean on a stone fence and watch. Towards the river, a woman spreads dirt on a field while a man plows an adjacent plot with two water buffalo. Alternating staccato chants with sharp whistles. Moving closer to the man, I watch him squat down, hammer his plow with a rock to tighten a joint, replace the rock on the ground, blow his nose out with his fingers, stand up again. I catch myself inwardly repeat these movement gestures. I am the plowman and I assess the day from his point of view. For the moment, I don't feel like a stranger.

We come to a farmhouse. Children run out to greet us. Another traveler passes, a man with a small handbag. He engages us in conversation, asks where we are going. He tells us not to go there. Maybe it's another warning. But the children remain stationed around us, and when I look into their faces, I feel protected. I want to explore further.

On the edge of this small settlement, atop a steep incline, above a grove of trees shimmering with golden autumn leaves, we see a small Tibetan style monastery. We are drawn there and soon arrive at the entrance to Pilling village. A man sits on the ground in front of prayer wheels made of old tin powdered milk cans painted blue and orange. He greets us with child-like gestures. When he leads us through a maze of houses, I assume he is guiding us to the monastery. I see this as auspicious. We're being led to a pre-destined rendezvous. We follow him expectantly. After winding through the maze of houses and outbuildings, he ends up back at his spot in front of the prayer wheels. When we realize we have gone round in a big circle, Lauren and I laugh at ourselves, but we're also disappointed. We wander about on our own and then suddenly, out of nowhere, a covey of small children appear, hands outstretched, chanting, "Mithai, mithai." I stick out my hand in imitation of them and repeat this familiar request for sweets. They smile and laugh. Two older children poke their heads out the gate of a nearby compound. They don't smile, and the little ones fall silent.

We all stand like this for what seems like forever. I ponder the prophesies of this day. Up to this point I've been alternating between apprehension and confidence. I'm just not sure how to read the signs.

I'm still wondering about it, when a man with an air of authority appears and joins the circle. I greet him and ask him about the village. My language. His language.

It's slow going. And much of what we say is not understood by either of us. When he squats down, I take this as the signal I've been waiting for and I also squat down. *"Gompa."* "Monastery," I say, pointing above the village to billowing prayer flags then to myself, to him, and back to the prayer flags.

Minutes later, he is leading us through cobblestone streets, uphill to a small red structure which is the new Pilling monastery. On the way in, in a small, dimly lit room, I see an old lama dressed in the style of the region: long braids wound up under a wide domed dark cloth hat; heavy skirts, fur trimmed jacket, and short, patterned leather boots. He joins us and while he spins his prayer wheel, he seems to occupy no space at all and the whole room at once. His companion, a lay monk, takes a pointer, and in a loud voice, eagerly names the figures in dark *thangkas*, the traditional scrolled paintings. He is delighted that I recognize some of them, know their names.

The old lama, who up to this moment has said nothing, now brings out photographs of his contemporary Buddhist teachers, all of whom I've met. To me this is an extraordinary coincidence, but neither the monk nor the lama is surprised.

Now we're led to the old monastery, the one we saw at the edge of the settlement. From below, it glowed in the sun, but inside it is so musty and dark, the frescoes on walls and cabinets are barely visible. The traditional statues—*rupas*—sit on a shelf above the cabinets. *They* can be seen *and* felt. All this time, the old man spins his prayer wheel and moves his mouth, smiles from time to time, and speaks soft low sentences in the local Tibetan dialect. I feel like I could stand here forever.

When we leave, it's partly because there is nothing more to say. With the wind likely to kick up, I remember the trail back.

Under this spell of enchantment, we head back down the same autumn slope to the river. Wind whipping sand and pebbles around. For some reason, the enchantment perhaps, we attempt to ford the river. We work our way around and around until it's clear we just can't do it. I see a pony caravan traversing the water. I want to call out to offer money for a ride back across, but I don't have the energy to make myself heard. I am spent in wind and walk.

November 8

Our porters, Mona and Dil, the young men I hired in Pokhara, arrive exactly on time, hungry and delighted to find us. But Mona has bad blisters. Following the recommended protocol, I had determined that they both had adequate clothing and shoes. But it turns out, his shoes are too small. Later in the day, after a four hour hike to Jharkot, his blisters worsen and I treat them with iodine and bandages. Since we are stopping for two nights, he is told to stay put, no walking.

Jharkot is another medieval town. Not many people stop here because forty minutes further on is a strip of restaurants and lodges, a party place for young trekkers, saucer-eyed, coming down from the great, seventeen thousand foot Thorung-la pass.

It's full moon, the most auspicious time to visit the sacred temples. I've asked about special full moon feast practices and the responses have been affirmative yet unspecific. It's a question of language, names and designations. A town for instance, has one name on the map, another name when you inquire, and yet another among the people themselves. And there are different versions of all the different names—official ones, historical ones, religious ones, caste, and folk names. Here, discovery is left to coincidence.

It's a brief but steep climb to Muktinath. We passed and were passed by Europeans with lightweight cross-country walking poles and by organized groups with overloaded porters. These small, powerful men carry baskets with a hundred and more pounds of equipment, and are propelled downhill by the weight.

At the entrance to the Muktinath temple compound, an old woman guards a huge, primitive prayer wheel. She hisses, beckons, and solicits payment. When I start to turn the first of a hundred smaller homemade prayer wheels, I feel suddenly vulnerable. Sure enough, the hag comes after me, arms flying. She doesn't like the way I'm doing it, a perfect excuse to ask for more money, jarring the openness I've begun to feel while turning the prayer wheels. Now, I move away quickly.

I enter the Muktinath Darshan Memorial Garden. Established in 1992 it contains young shrubs and trees staked and marked with names and addresses of donors from all over the world. I read familiar street names from Amsterdam, Berlin, London, San Francisco, New York. This international display high up in the Himalaya moves me deeply. The idea of us all crossing paths in a remote and sparsely populated corner of the globe, in a memorial garden, brings tears to my eyes. I walk across the garden to the Hindu pagoda shrine, where people are receiving cinnabar *tikka*, Hindu blessings, on their foreheads.

Up here it doesn't matter so much who is Hindu, Buddhist, Bonpo; what sect or lineage. Buddhist prayer flags are strung throughout and behind the pagoda temple, in a semi-circle, one hundred and eight water spouts, in shapes of mythical animal heads, spill water offerings onto the ground.

I enter a Buddhist monastery where a group of people are performing a *puja*. They chant and drum and ring bells. Two women make offerings to the shrine and pass around tea and small cakes. The leader is a young lama—long black braids, earrings, skirts—it's a funeral practice for his grandfather. In the middle is the same lay monk I asked about the feast practice back at the lodge. At the other end of the *puja* tables, a woman chants in a rich contralto with a nasal trill. I recognize her from Jharkot. Yesterday, I wandered into her house, thinking it was the Jharkot monastery, and this morning we waved to each other as she walked up the trail. Here we are, together at the feast practice. It was left to me to find my way.

November 9

I am awakened by a knock on my door and a voice saying
"Your friend is sick," I go down to the courtyard where Lauren is
vomiting. She's been sick like this all night—fever, diarrhea,
chills. Now she's dizzy and she might be hallucinating. I grab
my chart on altitude sickness and confer with the man who
knocked on my door, an experienced sherpa.

According to the categories, Lauren's symptoms are
neither mild nor severe, but moderate. The sherpa says flatly
the only thing to do is take her down, see if she improves. I
pack up her stuff and prepare Dil, the gentler of our two
porters, to go with her. She can hardly move but she's concerned about leaving the residue of her sickness in the room. I
assure her these people have seen it before. After they set
out, I talk further with the sherpa. He assures me that altitude
sickness can happen to anyone above seven or eight thousand feet. I'm comforted by his matter-of-factness.

When Mona and I first catch up to Lauren and Dil on the
trail she is not much better. I take my place on her right side,
Dil on her left. That helps her pace. She rests every ten or
fifteen minutes, just flops down. Still feverish, still short of
breath. As we continue, my thought is to synchronize our

71

steps, to send fresh breath into her system. After two hours, her gait shifts. She is more steady on her feet, resting less frequently, able to drink more than just sips of water. Then the last hour, descending the last of thirty-five hundred feet, she walks by herself. It's true. The descent makes all the difference. Released, I bound down to find us rooms in the way station of Eklabatti, which means in local dialect, *"Lonely Inn."* Tucked into bed in the Hilton Lodge, Lauren is smiling—quiet, graceful, a spirit reborn. After that, she's asleep for the next eighteen hours.

What I think about in the outpost of Eklabatti: what to do for the next six hours of daylight here at the Hilton Inn; the wind off the river beds, battering, rattling the glass windows, dust and debris swirling everywhere, greasy food, dirty rooms, the prospect of all these hours alone with Mona and Dil—like Larry McMurtry's novel *Lonesome Dove*, translated into Nepali.

I play carom, the national board game, with the porters. You flick a checker sized puck with your fingers, trying to strategically place it in the opponent's court. Just as my claustrophobia begins to peak, there's a tapping on the front window and I look out to see my friend Charles Ramble, a British anthropologist from Kathmandu, holding the reins of his horse and smiling. I'm astounded at this apparition.

In he strides, snappy scarf around sunburned neck, high leather spats buckled over riding boots, vest and tinted glasses, blond hair perfectly distressed. A vision from an early aviation newsreel. A half hour later, he's gone, and I'm still piecing it together. He sought me out in Jharkot, heard I'd left for Kagbeni, stopped there, then figured out Eklabatti. He's full of great friendly greetings, just out and about, flew up, got his horse, saying hello to friends, checking out projects, can't stay.

Charles orders *rakshi*, the local brandy, for everyone. Of course, it's the perfect thing to do just now in Eklabatti. I roll a cigarette from his pouch of tobacco. I just want to sit and drink and smoke and talk. By the time Charles is leaving, all I want to do is go with him. Just get a horse from the corral next door, leave word for Lauren that I'll be back in a day or two, and go. But how can I leave her here? Instead, I walk with Charles to his horse, we exchange greetings, and I watch him ride off, literally, at a gallop. Mona, Dil and I go across the street to another empty hotel and look through stacks of postcards. I hold in my hand small photographs of dazzling Himalayan peaks. There is no way to assess the gorgeous desolation. This land, these hundreds of years of herders, farmers, Bonpos, Buddhists. They remain for the moment, but for how much longer?

At two A.M. over the Hilton Lodge in Eklabatti, a full moon wash of limestone spreads over the landscape. I lie awake for hours, feeling and thinking, *"empty, empty."* Each barren night, each mud stone room, comfort here is sun on brown hills, on white rocks. The sole luxury is the opulent peaks—gatekeepers to another realm.

And plumage that decorates donkeys. The way ponies shimmer in woven blankets, braided tails. Last plateaus, songs of last Himalayan farmers, bells of warning sounded on high paths. Inexpressible fertility of space. I watch my heart—a lens—open, shut, open, shut. And the girls washes washes and the boys same same. And the girls washes washes and the boys same same. Blow noses with fingers, wipe asses with fingers, eat rice with fingers. Washes washes. Same same.

Tonight, I watch the young lodge woman sweep the floors. Undisturbed, she hums softly to herself. Washes washes. Same same.

November 10

The day washes through. Lauren is back from the dead and we wander for eight hours from Eklabatti to Marpha. We need to lose our way again, plow into the day's heavy clouds, into the wonders of high mountain agriculture, swinging suspension bridges, interminable stone steps, all this along the gorge at eighty-five hundred feet. In the end, we hobble over fields and fields of river rocks until we're sorry and hungry. We reach Marpha at dusk. The lodge we choose turns out to be filled with yak, their stench, and tracks of blood in the hallway.

We are alone here. There are no other guests. Marpha is populated by Thakali people, some of them descendants of wealthy merchants of the ancient great salt route, known for their proud, sharp trading, for their rapid fire speech. The porters balked at staying here. They'd been turned out when they arrived by themselves. Only with us are they allowed to stay.

It's late now and quiet. I am the last one around the fire. The grandparents have moved into their bed in the storeroom. The young son has fallen asleep on the floor cushions his grandfather vacated. His little sister, after chopping vegetables, went to sleep in a makeshift bed in the corner two hours ago while the chattering was still loud. The mother is still working on yak parts in the kitchen. The baby was put down somewhere.

I've been reading, drinking apple brandy, listening in to conversations in a language I don't understand. Absorbed.

Content in silence. Wrapped in it. Like the day's trek wrapped me in wind blown terrain.

Grandma is back in her chair, her gray-black hair shines, braids tied in circles to a bun at the back of her neck. She seems implacable—arms and hands covered in bracelets and rings of heavy turquoise and coral, necklaces of various sizes. Across from her, comfortable, I sit in five layers of clothing. The mother appears, removes her head scarf, and smiles faintly for the first time. The singing clock ticks. The wind and the river howl together.

The fire is re-filled one last time. I experience the humility of tenderness—penetrating, simple. I have no history. I'm sitting in the bones of now.

November 11

It's drizzling harder and harder as we do a few errands around Marpha. Donkey trains clatter through narrow slate streets and alleyways. In the next town, Thukche, we hope to see the annual lama dances.

Out on the trail it's raining hard. Deep ruts fill with water. We had plans to scout out an experimental farm station and a

Tibetan refugee settlement, but as the road turns to mud, we dig in and just walk through the downpour.

It rains and rains and rains. Twenty-four hours in all and still strong clouds blow from both ranges south and north across the narrow valley. Later we hear that it rained and snowed all over Nepal, a freak storm whose sudden heavy snow caused avalanches, destroying a whole town on the eastern Annapurna slope. We are uncertain whether the lama dances can go on or not, but as the preliminaries are set up, the sun appears.

This little monastery was moved from the other side of the river ten years ago. Krishna, one of three brothers who has returned here for their mother's funeral, tells me this. He watched me writing in my journal, approached me, and asked me to transcribe the story of the event.

The dance is the story of how Padmasambhava, Guru Rinpoche, came to Tibet to build the Samye Ling monastery. It's performed like this annually in certain monasteries throughout the Nepal Himalaya. As the performance begins, we take our places huddled together on piles of straw in a square arena packed with folks from the greater region. Small tribes of children cavort about, then return to the women for food and comfort. Men stand about, smoking, talking. More than anything, it's like an old-fashioned, small town circus inside a courtyard.

The performance is about good and evil, about devotion, power, and magic. It invokes the four directions, the five elements and the power of the *dakini*, the female deity energy of awareness. During wild interludes, buffoon characters of graveyard demons and monkeys, hurl themselves into the audience. Old women are toppled by these human projectiles. Nobody is spared. Now the children are frightened and they move close to the elders and tuck themselves under the womens' heavy shawls and blankets.

I am honored to be the scribe. It's hard work, compounded by Krishna's spotty English, by the complexity of the story, and by the repetitive entrances and movements of the characters. But I am no longer just a tourist. For the moment, I hold a place in the ceremony.

I am honored to be with these three brothers whose father was the lama of Thukche, whose family claims descent from the great yogi Milarepa, Tibet's national poet and saint.

During one of the many pauses, Krishna takes me across the street to a basement room that's operating today as a restaurant. I'm offered a plate of lightly grilled yak meat but defer, asking instead for a bowl of rice. When the homemade beer comes around, I sip gingerly and celebrate the occasion.

On departure the next morning, all three Thukche brothers take us down the road, down an alley, to the family monastery. Its impression, its scale, is like a medieval chapel. They tease me that I knew them in a previous life; that I am the incarnation of their great uncle, an enlightened lama; that I must stay and be the lama for their family monastery.

I imagine the three of them, Krishna, Chakra, Sashi, growing up in this town. When I watch them pose for a photograph, three middle-aged figures, same height, same open faces, I think—the Marx Brothers. Then I think, maybe I *was* in their former life.

November 13

Leaving Thukche we hit terrific winds. At Larjung, where we cross a wide branch of the Kali Gandaki River, the dust whips and stings against exposed flesh, and for the first time I'm glad to be surrounded by a pack of European trekkers and their guides.

Everyone is covered with scarves, bandannas, sunglasses, hoods; plunging across the divide, pushing against the wind. On the other side, we are suddenly in pine forest, winding up and down along the river, glancing through trees at snow peaks as the gorge narrows again.

We've entered the area where dramatic changes in climate occur every few hours. The temperature rises and falls, we move from full sun to full shadow, the winds kick up and settle back down. Throughout these changes I adopt a personal ritual for taking off and putting on clothing while continuing to walk.

I pull down my hood, untie my bandanna, my face scarf, stuff them into jacket pockets, zip up the pockets. Take off the jacket, tie the sleeves around my waist, double knot over waist pack. Fold shirt collar down, unbutton top buttons, roll up shirt sleeves, push up long underwear sleeves. Ah, breeze through body.

Around the ridge, gusts come up. Roll down sleeves, careful to hold long underwear sleeves in place. Button up shirt, collar up. Untie jacket, walking cautiously now, slip on one arm then the other. Snap four snaps, pull up hood, unzip jacket pockets, remove bandanna and scarf. Replace sunglasses, tie bandanna around hood, wrap scarf over face.

I maneuver like this under the gaze of the great peaks of the Annapurna range. For the next six days, they are never out of sight for more than a few hours. They hover in gigantic shadow. Like new lovers, you can't help thinking about them all the time. And yet you can't really take them in unless you stop everything and focus.

These peaks range from twenty to twenty-four thousand feet. I become familiar with their names: Dhampus, Thuke, Dhauligiri in the north, the Nilgiri trio—north, central, south— and the inner peaks of the Annapurna Sanctuary—Himchuli, Lamjung Himal, sacred Machhapuchhare, Annapurna I-IV, Annapurna South.

Back up on the Lower Mustang plateau, the peaks stood close against stark brown hills and sheer ridges—windswept giants dazzling in sunlight. Here, lower down, they become distant and more companionable.

We stop for the night in Kalopani and at the far end of town, in the last hours of light, we play catch with children, variations of monkey in the middle and whoever can grab the ball. They have powerful throwing arms, natural, graceful movements, all of them—little ones to adolescents. And of course, since they never want to stop, the game continues until we're halfway back into town. In the last of the day we sit on a guest house terrace and watch the fading light transform the peaks.

Dhauligiri shadows. At night the wind howls and rattles the thin wood frames of the shack we sleep in. I dream of camel trains on giant sand dunes and wake covered in a film of dirt, the same thin deposit throughout the room.

November 15

A lush day of walking with many stops. Lete, Ghasa, Kopchepani, Rukse Chhaharo. Each town is dominated by a single ethnic group—Chetri, Gurung, Magar, Moghul. We come down to six thousand feet, entering a tropical terrain. Plum shaped tree tomatoes, blooming poinsettia trees, green, terraced mountain slopes, sub-alpine meadows, and all the way the Kali Gandaki surging, crashing under steep waterfalls.

Flower and vegetable gardens on both sides of the trail: cabbage, chard, squash, melons, pumpkins, gourds, hibiscus, tiger lilies, ornamental fruit trees. Christmas cactus, blooming from rock walls, create barriers between trails and gardens. There are ferns everywhere, tropical cactus, stands of bamboo, tall palm fronds, and thick vines. Against all this, the massive walls of the Annapurna Sanctuary guard the hidden inner slopes.

Yesterday, we spent the whole morning in Tatopani, a little Woodstock in the Himalayas. I soak in the hot springs, get a shave, clean myself up, and mingle with the international crowd. There's fresh squeezed orange juice, veggie burgers and cheesecake, lithium batteries in camera repair shops. It's a reality check for me when I change money in a bank, look at clothing in stores, and buy a new notebook. The interlude here contrasts so sharply with where we've come from. I could just crash here for a week.

From Tatopani we climb and descend the trail, up and down along thousands of stone steps. We enter rhododendron forests, storybook woods with gnarled and twisted shapes, the trail dark and slanted, full of birdsong and thick forest floor. Then up and up, back up to Ghorepani at nine thousand feet with sore shins and what feels like the last of my legs. It's impossible to calculate distances when most of a day is spent moving up and down, crossing and re-crossing sides of mountain slopes. Today, I drink hot ginger water at every teahouse to keep up my strength and spirits.

Ghorepani is famous among tourists for a pre-dawn trek, twelve hundred feet up to Poon Hill, where you can watch the sun rise and gradually illumine a circle of snow peaks as day breaks. We stay at the Moonlight Lodge perched high above the town. Along with every trekker, we get up at five A.M. and make the climb. It's a vigil—all of us bunched together at the top, on the rise of a small crest. It begins to feel like a peace march.

The first rays appear and then all manner of camera equipment goes into motion, trying to catch the extended play of light and peaks, which slowly fills the whole circle with glorious sun. In this gorgeous crescendo, I am shocked by the sound and action, the attempt to grasp and record the moment. But I too am recording. How mixed my feelings are: tension, ambivalence, self-questioning.

On the way down, I walk with one of the local men who brought the coffee concession up the hill, and engage him in conversation. At first, I'm all too aware that I'm pushing myself to reconnect, trying to ground myself again by talking. But gradually, I relax into the rhythm of the conversation, the fragments of ideas we exchange, the details of the life of the village. It's the commitment to the exchange that brings me back.

After the climb up and down, I'm exhausted. I never really recovered from yesterday. The morning is bittersweet. Today will be a short walking day. In mid-afternoon, we stop at

Banthati, with its five lodges thrown together along a ravine, backed up against a steep mountain wall. Already we're losing the sun, and after a long nap, it's cold and nearly dark. Small goats wander in and out of the dining room and kitchen. The rooms are filthy and the lodge owners gruff. I sleep twelve hours and in the morning, when the lodge owner jokes with me, I find her a more reasonable human being.

November 17

On the outskirts of Ghandruk, the last village we sleep in, we are greeted by a shy group of children whose mother stands nearby. I take this return of children as a good sign heralding comfort and good food. And it is a good sign. Ghandruk is a beautiful place, set on a series of hills. It has a plan to it. Landscaped, stone paths lead everywhere and through foliage, one glimpses well-designed farmhouses with stone patios and formal entryways.

Every turn of the way holds views of vast terraced hillsides, mixed with slices of domestic life—sorting rice, stocking feed bins, weaving rugs, plaiting bamboo mats, scrubbing, washing. Here, the Annapurna Conservation Project has added to the pride and commitment of the villagers. There is a municipal compost and designated sanitation areas. Solar generators, kerosene stoves, a day care center, women's groups. And though the ancient culture of the high Himalaya is days behind us, there is grace in Ghandruk, when I really need it.

It's my forty-ninth birthday. In Nepal, the concept of a personal birthday does not exist. People celebrate the birth of the country. Nonetheless, I take my celebration in the refined pleasure of the place, in one last, long afternoon of playing pied piper to a spontaneously formed gang of village kids.

November 19

On the way down, I feel weightless. It's not just the magnificence of the scenery, but the fact that the trail is relatively flat and open, so I can walk and look out in both directions. I'm aware of all the new sensations that have become part of who I am. I'm taking this with me.

On the way down, a young farmer catches up to me and within moments we are walking with arms around each other's shoulders, conversing about our lives. When he leaves, he carefully writes his name and address in my book in an elaborate Hindi script. We wave to each other for the next half mile until he disappears over a hill.

On the way down, schoolchildren returning home stop and ask to have their picture taken. In this last afternoon walk, nothing seems out of place. My mind cradles the landscape. My body speaks its rhythm. Sings to it, devoted to the space of all of it.

On the way down, I am blessed by the magic of the great Himalayas.

Map of the City of Kathmandu

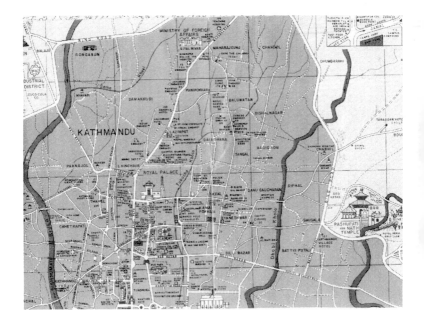

3

KATHMANDU,
THREE YEARS LATER

Within three months of my return from Asia, I was longing to go back. I thought constantly about Nepal as I edited my journals and presented slide shows. It wasn't the travel so much, although the somatic memory of trekking was with me whenever I hiked. I also remembered the feeling I'd had about myself, the way concept and self-image had shifted while I was in Nepal.

Each autumn and spring for the next few years, I tried to arrange to return, but work and major transitions postponed any travel plans. Then I remembered that the Venerable Thrangu Rinpoche teaches an annual seminar at his monastery in Boudnath, Kathmandu. When I called for further information, I was told about a pilgrimage that Rinpoche was leading—a retreat in a cave of Guru Rinpoche—Padmasambhava—high in the foothills, in the sacred Yolmo valley. I phoned the travel agent that same day. Several weeks later, I was telling my good friend Wendell Beavers about my plans, and on the spot, he decided to accompany me. These were auspicious beginnings for my return.

March 14

Everything is so familiar. Of course I've thought so much about the place and the people these last three years—like a lost love. Changes seem minimal—a restaurant here, a hotel there, a new monastery, a small high rise. What used to be ISD/STD/FAX—mail and phone services—now includes INTERNET, and the e-mail is cheap and almost reliable. The towering construction on the horizon separating two neighborhoods—Boudha and Chahubil—is an international hotel mocking a traditional palace style, lavishly built, surrounded by shacks and bumpy dirt roads.

We were fortunate in Singapore to be seated in business class for the last leg. It made all the difference—a deep sleep, good full portions of food and room to stretch out, breathe, be served. And fortunate to see the whole range of the Himalayas for the last half hour of the flight—a spell cast over the passengers that transforms all of us into adventurers. Fully and quickly, I've left everything behind, happy to be on the road, to have obligations only to listen to dharma, to roam the Kathmandu Valley, and to guide my friend Wendell on his first journey to Asia.

94

We are the first ones through customs and out the door. Ani-la, a Tibetan nun and friend, is waiting for us as soon as we are out and wants to carry our luggage. We are so pleased to see each other that it crosses my mind how it's hard not to hug a nun. We exchange continuous bows of greeting accompanied by short statements about arrival. *"Can you get a taxi?"* sinks in, and she is soon back with a too small car preceded by six guys elbowing each other to get to our luggage. Ani-la settles the fare, the guys load the luggage, it doesn't fit, we get another taxi, re-load, I give out tips, and despite the sudden disorientation of arrival after thirty-two hours in three airplanes and four airports, and the devastating reality of the Kathmandu air, we are off into incredible dust and pollution.

On the drive from the airport, we pass long stretches of ramshackle shops and huts before any organized district appears. The small airport has its own kind of 1960s integrity, but what first meets the eye of the traveler on the main road to town is an astonishing disorder of humans, animals and commodities. And the final stretch into Boudha on the Mahankal road deserves a Land Rover, not the twenty year old economy car we are riding in. So we arrive at Rabsel Guest House nearly speechless and Ani-la gets two construction workers to carry our bags while she goes to get bottled water.

low stools with sacks of twisted fried bread sticks or flat doughy muffins on the ground in front of them. One boy stands behind small mounds of spices heaped onto a plastic sheet, another with open bags of grains. The thermos sellers are unpacking and slowly the doors and gates of shops lift and roll open while various wares are set out in front of them.

The new thing around the Stupa is makeshift plywood tables with suitcases filled with white shirts, shifts and fabrics propped open and set out. These concessions form a ring within arm's length of the circumambulating path. The goods are from China. I find both these facts ironic and disturbing.

Later in the day we go to Thrangu Rinpoche's monastery, Thrangu Tashi Choling, and sit in a modest sized shrine room, comfortable enough for the sixty people who attend the seminar. The room faces the Great Stupa, seen in shadow through curtains drawn against the sun, windows open to catch breezes. Our schedule for the Namo Buddha Seminar is simple—teachings in the morning, preceded by an optional meditation period. In the afternoon, we will meet several times a week to study for the retreat and pilgrimage to the Langtang Valley north of Kathmandu that some of us will make after the seminar. This annual three week seminar is based on a particular Mahamudra text, written in the eleventh century by eventually it was too much. We began with Dawa's antique shop on Durbar Marg, then the bookstores and music stores around the corner. Started up the steep road to Lazimpat to see the sleeping bats, but waves of heat pushed us back. Then before I knew it, we were walking towards Thamel, into hundreds of shops in a tourist's labyrinth. Some kind of magnetic field drew me on until I was overwhelmed. I have this experience in places I've loved where I need to turn every corner, flush out every old story and in the end, though the mood is flattened by speed and compression, I am again familiar.

I'm touched by the easy way people remember me. A few shopkeepers greet me by name. They hold their hands together in prayer position, look me in the eye, then say my name and clasp my hands. Others examine me for a while before they make the connection. In contacts here, there is something deeper than I experience at home, more old-fashioned—like the way you imagine people in a small town relating to you after you've been away for years. Or in fact, where I grew up, the old ones still call me Stevie and in their eyes I watch them remember me as a child.

What is it about memory—about time and relation-ships—that works this way?

I've learned that in Nepal, time does not move in a linear way. A way of recalling exists that makes me feel instantly at home. Familiarity, repeated contact, expands the notion of time—mixes it with space, with situations—and encourages an ongoing circular exchange.

March 18

___

At 5:30 in the morning nobody is stirring. A few Tibetans move towards the Stupa, but most people are just waking in the first light of day. The dogs in the night were piercing and erratic. At the first outburst, I put my earplugs in. A dog on the roof next door, now sweet and serene, reminds me of this as I look at her silhouette against the sky. The light between 6:15 and 6:45 in the morning is so soft on the brown rounded hills surrounding the valley. It feels sensual here—immediately. What took months to acknowledge the last time. Still, I'm talking myself through a shift of letting go the past and establishing the present.

By the time I get to the Stupa to join the circumambulating, the sun is hazy and the pollution so strong that my eyes are running. I'm sneezing and feeling groggy. I hear it hasn't that he seems oblivious to his surroundings. This morning, a few Tibetan women have coaxed him to the front of their shop. They offer him cereal and tea. He lays the food out on the ground and eats one piece at a time, chewing slowly, vigorously, his unfocused eyes wandering. Yesterday he was naked until someone bought him a long tee-shirt. Today the tee-shirt is stained and blackened. I think of Chime, my street woman friend from three years ago. She's dead now. But her lineage of social misfits continues to seek shelter at the Stupa.

What interests me in the morning *kora* is the vulnerability I feel walking among the people here—the directness of offering prayers, *mantra*, or in this case, simply participating in daily life, sharing in others' lives. Reciting *mantras* joins one to others' suffering, one's aspirations to those of all people. The power of chanting, intoning, is that simple and that direct.

Both the vulnerability and the empowerment are the reflective mirrors that *sangha*—the community—provides. Around the Stupa, the villagers are *sangha*, and all beings and activities are contained—beggars, crippled and deformed, wild dogs, tourists, the trademark pigeons fed each day on the slopes of the Stupa walls. Morning is the more direct, fresh time. By evening, the crowd is full of tourists and with the light fading, everything becomes soft, surreal, almost nostalgic.

102

In one of my rounds of circle walking, I watch two old women eye a discarded towel on the ground. They've paused, and now they exchange several long questioning glances until one of them picks it up and they continue walking and spinning their prayer wheels. Tibetans here are cautious like this, but they also do what they want. They remind me of my grandparents' generation of Russian Jewish refugees in New York.

What's different about this visit is that living in the Rabsel Guest House at Sechen Monastery instead of in the self-contained compound of the study abroad program with its own kitchen staff, we rely on restaurants for all our meals. Gradually we are invited to more and more lunches and dinners with friends, but for now, we alternate between the Stupa View Restaurant and the new Three Sisters.

At best, service is whimsical. You can place bets on how long it will be until someone takes your order or when the food will arrive. In the morning, since they barely start serving at eight, it's a close call to get to the meditation session on time. At either place, waiting for a side dish or a second cup of coffee is anybody's guess. On several occasions, I pay the bill and leave without these extras.

By eight in the morning at the Stupa View Restaurant, the chefs and apprentices are in their white hats and jackets, officiating in the kitchen, but the waiters and busboys are so magnetized by these kitchen rituals, they seem to forget the customers. They are happy to be reminded as though it's the very thing they've been waiting for.

On the other hand, at the less formal Three Sisters Restaurant, the young waiter is almost deadpan in his neglect. When he finally takes my order, he can't believe that I want fruit salad and yogurt along with French toast. As I spread the yogurt and fruit on the fried bread, he watches me in absolute amazement.

March 19

It's seven in the morning. I know by the cry of the man selling potatoes from his bicycle as he moves along the street. I'm sure he's saying *"potatoes, potatoes"* as I catch a glimpse of him out my window, but he could be saying anything. I have no knowledge of Nepali or Tibetan. I speak in signs and gestures which combined with slow, dramatic, and carefully constructed English words convey my meaning. Theirs I intuit by their response, and by whether the attempted exchange succeeds. If it doesn't, I try again, using the incomplete first attempt as a working basis.

As the potato seller moves out of sight, I notice the carpet factory across the street is in full swing. On a concrete patio the size of a basketball court, half a dozen men sweep water and soap out of the carpets, while half a dozen others stand around waiting for the next step in the process. The cleaning is long—several times of dyeing, washing, drying. It's heavy work, and like manual labor in Nepal, slow, repetitive, seemingly endless.

When I leave the guest house, I see that the monks at Sechen Monastery have come out of a nine day *puja*. Up until now, the only time I've seen them is in the evening when they practice the lama dances they will perform next week. We watch them from the courtyard entrance on our way home in the evening. The dance movements consist of high lifts of one leg, a pivot on the standing leg, a small turn, then a lift of the other leg. Wearing long, maroon robes makes it look and, I imagine, feel quite different. Each set of movements is symmetrical and the dance moves in circles.

In Tibetan Buddhism the circle image is elaborated in the iconography of the *mandala*, a sacred circular or disk enclosure which creates a symbolic transformation of the universe from a place of suffering to a place of happiness. Considering the *mandala* principle in relation to the sacred dances, I understand how the Tibetan dance tradition is a way of celebrating the victory of enlightenment over darkness. Those initiated—lamas and monks—hold the responsibility to communicate this message through the performance.

March 21

We walked up to Pullihari Monastery on our first day off from the seminar. It's a one hour walk at a leisurely pace, a little longer if you stop and talk to school children along the way or look at vegetable gardens. I've been looking forward to this visit for a year now, since I heard that the reincarnation of the third Jamgon Kongtrul Rinpoche had been discovered. Pullihari Monastery is his seat; he is now the fourth Jamgon Kongtrul Rinpoche. This incarnation was found in Tibet, according to signs and descriptions, judiciously brought to Nepal, and installed at the age of two. In the tradition of reincarnate teachers, accomplished masters have overseen his confirmation and enthronement. Now he is almost three and already there are many stories about his intelligence and compassion.

His eyes are large and bright and his face has the great, soft, sweet feeling of his predecessor. When I watch him in action, posing for photographs on his throne cushions and playing with things around him, I feel his specialness, the determination and seriousness that he carries.

His general secretary, who has been administering Pullihari's international activities these past eight years of Jamgon Kongtrul's absence, continues to serve the new, young Rinpoche. The boy's tutor is a monk who was in the circle of students of the previous Rinpoche. The oldest monk at Pullihari is now serving his third Jamgon Kongtrul incarnation. They provide a perfect example of the principles of lineage and mandala at work.

We enter the room to offer *katas* to the three year old Rinpoche. He sits upright, in a maroon sweat suit, with a stuffed Mickey Mouse, taller than himself, next to him. I remember my relationship to his predecessor. I hold back tears when the boy places his little hand in blessing on top of my head. Finished with this duty, he scrambles down and goes off to investigate the world. Everyone is gentle with him but also firm. At one point, a workman moves him out of the way, but a minute later they let him climb to the top of a high ladder with some tools, imitating their work. When one of his attendants asks if we'd like to take some photographs,

Rinpoche gets back up on his throne and poses until we are satisfied. Then he walks over to a railing, picks up his bib, and puts it around his neck, signaling his lunch time.

March 22

I wake up to the potato man and to blessings from yesterday's visit to Pullihari. When I feel the blessings, I think of my mother. In two days it will be the first anniversary of her death. After she died, I sent a letter to Pullihari so she could be included in their prayer practice for the deceased. Yesterday, one of the administrators reminded me of that and asked if I wanted to write down names of others, both dying, and ill, to be included in the monks' daily prayers. Here was an opportunity to join ill friends to a tradition that honors both dying and healing in a formal and functional way. The prayers are meant to pacify and guide one's mind in the midst of the dying process, and in the case of the deceased, to assist one's rebirth. Writing down a list of names guides my thoughts to friends with life threatening illnesses. The path of these thoughts is more clear in this culture where impermanence is deeply felt in daily life and where human relationships can be unfettered and more gentle.

108

March 23

Another Stupa morning. These past two days I am full of tears; they just come and go all morning, and ease up after that. They catch me by surprise, but after all, tomorrow is the day my mother died one year ago.

The Mahamudra teachings that we are studying in Thrangu Rinpoche's seminar resonate. The teachings join the mindfulness and awareness practices of meditation. I've studied and practiced this way for twenty-five years, but I am always re-examining the fundamentals. Here, I can listen with barely any distraction, and because there is so little else on my mind, I can sense the activity of this listening as I move through the day. Again, I'm reminded that Tulku Urgyen Rinpoche spoke about the accumulation of glimpses of clarity/awareness as a gradual path to enlightenment.

Another Stupa morning. Eating breakfast feels like the movie *Groundhog Day*. At Three Sisters, the personnel never changes, and the waiter affects precisely the same indifference every day. And Wendell and I ask each other in the same self-mocking tones, "*Eggs, French toast, or pancakes?*"

Today, the crowd formations in the morning *kora* catch my attention. There are two groups of elderly women, same size, four across, covered head to toe in muted cotton and wool clothing, with red and blue ribbons wound into long gray braids down their backs. There is a group of young Tibetan sharpies, mustaches, goatees, long black hair combed straight back. They amble along until they stop to slouch and light cigarettes in front of a shop. I imagine they've all seen the same James Dean poster.

The boy who delivers sacks of flour and produce pauses to catch his breath. Over and over he walks quickly with small boy steps back and forth around the Stupa, weighed down by his sacks, but still emanating pride and determination. He rarely glances up. Even on his empty—handed return trip, he doggedly pursues his course.

This morning I gave a jacket to the man with the hangdog expression who approaches me every day and formally shakes my hand just as he did three years ago. His expression makes my heart ache, even though he is conning me. From the two suitcases of clothes I brought to give to schools, I've saved this jacket for him. It's perfect, not just because it fits him, but because my Brazilian tenant left it behind in a closet two years ago. I like that this simple suede jacket has arrived on its third continent.

The possessed dancing lady is calm today, her fifth day of

public display. She has changed clothes and for some reason she's wiped red *sindura* paste on her face. She stands at the entrance gate saying prayers, lighting butter lamps. The regulars still watch her carefully, waiting for the next episode. Yesterday she sashayed around the Stupa, singing and taunting, her bare breasts cupped in her hands.

March 24

There is some perverse magic I feel in going downtown, getting out in traffic and moving along crowded dusty streets. I grew up in a city and I've always been attracted to that pulse. Here I love finding my way again, being drawn down a passageway I haven't seen before, never tiring of the potential adventure. Boudha is such a small place, really, just a few neighborhoods. Downtown the streets and quarters are each entirely different, like any other city.

The Durbar Square open air market is a favorite haunt of mine at dusk. Typically, I just find my way there. Where others might look forward to a cup of tea on a terrace, I strategize the late afternoon so that as the light fades I wind up in this open bazaar at closing time. The vendors sidle in furtively and intone their sales pitch: *"Few sale today, everything half."* *"Last closing, last selling.*" And the insinuating line which always gets me to respond, "*What you like?*"

I try to explain that I don't know what I like until I see it—that's the point of scanning like this—to seek out what I like. The vendors follow me around undaunted, offering up one piece after another. "*You like the Ganesh statue, no, okay, maybe you like brass dragon candle, this one very good one, very old, maybe you take both.*" I tell them I can see for myself, I know what is old, what is good, and further I know how much I want to pay. "*How much you pay?*"

I keep my head down, looking at items on the tables, items which repeat and repeat themselves. Occasionally, there is something that leaps out and I pick it up. When I hold it up to the fading light, a barrage of information begins, the introduction to the hard sell which attracts the attention of other vendors, and soon they are bringing the same exact object or variations of it for me to scrutinize. Suddenly, I remember this is the perfect way to do it, efficient, flushing out every possibility. The sellers are not competitive with each other, just pushy. In fact, if I start bargaining with one of them, others will join in and try to facilitate the deal. Maybe they tally up favors later.

As though the obscurity enhances my attention, I get pulled to what I like at the moment, to what I can barely see in the fading light. The shapes and images find their voice in the dusk in this mad twilight bardo, giving me an excuse to examine and imagine tiny objects, hammered, carved, created for a specific purpose. And the bargaining itself, at once tedious, electric, and theatrical, is like a blood cleanser to me.

By the time I'm through, it's night. The vendors have packed up and I am left alone—hungry, tired, looking for a taxi home. As I ride through interminable dark winding streets back to Boudha, the gestures and sounds of the marketplace ring in my head, the selling and buying like a ballroom dance tune.

March 25

_____

The *Kathmandu Post*, one of two English language dailies, proclaims its *"Outlook for Today"* under its headline logo: *"Fair throughout the Kingdom."* This is what it says every time I pick up the newspaper. Meanwhile, without a cleansing rain, the condition of the air continues to deteriorate. There is a flu epidemic in villages in the foothills which is killing hundreds of people and the government cannot mobilize its meager health care fast enough. A plane is sent back to Bangladesh, not because of the serious airport clashes over the Nepalese

113

pilots' strike, but because of smog conditions at the Kathmandu airport. As we walked home last night a light sprinkle fell for a few minutes and when we roused the night guard at the gate to Sechen Monastery, he reached his arms up to the drizzling sky and danced. *"Fair throughout the Kingdom."*

What is this acceleration in my body every day? At first I thought, same old thing—too many concerns on my mind— trying to mix study and practice with showing Wendell around Kathmandu, and shopping, negotiating, buying things. But this morning I have a different feeling which has been working in me the whole week and which just this morning I put into words—longing—a longing to understand these teachings and how to develop on the path. My feeling comes from the practice of wakeful clarity which is at the heart of the seminar. I experience an acceleration, both of practice and of desire to practice. It doesn't replace the other stuff—the desire for beautiful things, sex, health, good circumstances. It just shows them off in a different light.

We spent the afternoon doing meditation practice in the empty shrine room at Thrangu Rinpoche's monastery. I'd decided this was the simplest way to mark my mother's death. Wendell and I set up cushions in front of Rinpoche's throne seat and sat for two hours. It felt like Rinpoche was there; in fact, it felt like the entire Kagyu lineage of Buddhas and Bodhisattvas was there.

At the same time, what seems to work one day is different the next. Breakfast is delightful one day, unappealing the next. This morning's hot water lasts only thirty seconds instead of the usual five minutes. Every time I feel I've got a hold on something—digestion, sleep patterns, attire—it disintegrates—quickly.

March 26

Swayambunath is the other great stupa in Kathmandu. It stands on the highest spot in the valley and from that vantage point the entire city, perpetually clouded by smog, stretches out before you. Much of what is visible did not exist twenty years ago. The city has grown randomly, spread and filled in as the population and the demand for livelihood increases.

The Swayambunath Stupa is the place of the primordial Buddha, who is said to be without beginning and without end. As a reliquary, it holds an enduring and sacred flame. The Great Stupa of Dharmakaya (what I think of as "our" Stupa since it dominates our daily life in Boudnath) is conceived as the reliquary of the historic Shakyamuni Buddha, and holds some of his relics.

We wander around Swayambu in late afternoon light, just looking, photographing, sitting in one spot or another for long periods of time. It is unusually quiet, uncrowded, and has more the sense of a neighborhood than a tourist attraction. Schoolchildren play tag around the hundreds of small statues and shrines which occupy most of the area around the Stupa itself. Elderly monks sit against the base of a shrine and chat, working prayer beads with their fingers. Workmen chip away a three inch layer of plaster from the Stupa walls and the ground is covered in white dust. They work with ladders and picks, sometimes shifting their weight and placing a leg on the head of a sacred statue. A monk carries off a few chunks of plaster, then another monk does the same—as if they are carrying off souvenirs of the Berlin Wall.

Many monasteries, auxiliary shrines and temples surround Swayambunath Stupa. The area spreads out through woods full of monkeys and across descending ridges of an enormous hill. Little boy monks appear on the rooftop of their monastery and call down to us. They lean over the roof and the folds of their maroon robes decorate the ledge. Like the college boys of my first walk alone in Asan three years ago, they ask the obligatory questions: *"How are you?" "Where you are from?"* Even though they have words only for these simple repeated phrases, they are so playful and engaging. I lean against a wall and gaze up at them. After a while I take out my camera. Then they begin to pose. Walking away, I think there is no personal issue that the smile of a little boy monk cannot displace. Zen master, Suzuki Roshi once said, *"One kind word can turn over all of heaven and earth."*

In Boudha the Great Stupa of Dharmakaya is also being refurbished. At the base of the Stupa, five men stand hip deep in a pit filled with whitewash. They stir it with long paddles and then fill bucket after bucket and pass them up to another group of men. In turn, this team then passes the buckets up the dozens of steps that lead from one level of the Stupa to another. To get to the crown, where nobody climbs, the steps give way to niches, where a flat ladder has been placed and is held by strong hands so the climbers can reach the top. Stationed at the top, two men pour these pails of fresh whitewash down the sides of the wall. When it dries another team standing in the middle of the ladder flings pails of saffron colored powder upwards from where they are perched, to form the yellow lotus decoration. From close up in my

117

camera lens it seems remarkably imprecise, even sloppy. But from a distance, when it dries, the lotus effect is achieved.

Both the dancing woman and the deranged boy are absent this morning. The boy who delivers vegetables and grains pauses with his plastic bags. He's carrying too much. He rubs his wrist and his upper arm. Each set of bags is connected with a bandanna to make the carrying easier, but the boy is breathing hard and sweating. Today he's dressed in black nylon pants with white stripes down the side and a long black tee-shirt. On his next round he carries just one bag in each hand.

The produce sellers squat around the Stupa behind displays of carrots, lettuce, cabbage, scallions, eggplant, squash—laid out on plastic tarpaulins. Other sellers don't unload the produce, but place their wooden carrying yoke and wrought iron baskets down on the ground. The Tibetans who buy from them are fussy about what they pick out. They press and squeeze and handle the produce and examine the scale as things are weighed. Again, I'm reminded of immigrants in New York.

Today the sweepers are not pushing refuse and dust over the vegetables. And for some reason, the policewoman is helping with the sweeping. My curiosity to know why and how things like this occur is balanced by a strong hunch that there is no logic that would outlast the occurrence itself.

The spice boy stands perfectly straight and still behind a tall mound of cloves with a cup on top. His hands, covered in clear plastic gloves, dangle at his sides. He stays nearly motionless like this for long periods of time. Today I watch him take a break. He goes to have tea with his friend around the corner, the boy who stands behind two bushels of herbal twigs in burlap sacks.

March 28

A breezy afternoon with some cloud cover, becomes good news for hundreds of us who are gathered at Sechen Monastery for the annual Guru Rinpoche dances. Crowds line the balconies of the monks' quarters and the rooftops. All the grassy space on the ground and even the cement walkways are packed with Tibetans. Extended families sit on blankets eating picnic lunches, holding umbrellas, passing thermoses. Under an open tent on one side of the courtyard is the VIP area, only partly full, but you need a printed invitation to get in there. I'll wander from side to side of the arena and from upstairs to downstairs to have different vantage points and to feel out the crowd. For the next three hours I move from place to place, alternately watching and documenting the dances and taking portraits of the onlookers.

The process of shooting portraits becomes quickly interactive. Even the twenty foot distance of a telephoto lens does not prevent people from being immediately aware of the camera, as though they possess a heightened sensitivity to being photographed. It's rare that a person turns completely away, but many ignore me and just go on doing what they are doing—watching the dances, talking to friends, holding babies. Then it's up to me to maneuver for the shot, which is not easy in a tight crowd. Others invite the camera and pose, lifting their babies out in front of them or putting their arms around their companions' shoulders.

Moving up the stairs to the roof, I hold the camera over my head as I step over people squatting in the shade of the covered staircase. On the roof, the crowd is four and five deep, but in back of them children run and shout on the wide roof ledge and play games with sticks and stones. They pick up pebbles and toss them one at a time like marbles or in sequence like jacks. Twigs and sticks become archways and houses. Anything round is rolled back and forth. They simply pick up what's in front of them and play with that.

120

The sacred dances enact the establishment of Buddhism in Tibet. The dance pageant style is familiar to me now that I've witnessed it on several occasions. Unlike the museum pieces of the performance in the Himalayas three years ago, the brocade costumes and papier mache masks of these monks are newly made. Sechen is a well-endowed monastery of a major Tibetan teacher. One can't compare their training and resources to a small monastery in a traditional mountain village. Monasteries and nunneries are supported by the *sangha*, and by the teachings, activities, and services they perform. Monasteries like Sechen are supported as well by an international *sangha*, many of them Asians from Taiwan, Singapore, Malaysia, Hong Kong, some of them Westerners. The smaller village monasteries struggle to stay alive, as young people move to urban areas, and the traditions weaken from disuse.

The musicians sit under a tent decorated with dragons on the side of the arena facing the performers and the brightly painted and sculpted monastery entrance. It's a natural stage set. A massive saffron colored curtain covers the entire facade of the monastery creating a dramatic backdrop for the entrance down several dozen steps onto the floor of the arena. The crowd jeers and whistles at the *entr'actes* of clowns and buffoons who mock the ceremony and defuse its formality. Old people who have watched these pageants year after year all their lives, sit holding their grandchildren. Watching them I think about the Tibetan diaspora they are living through and wonder what they are thinking.

A long procession begins. Oversize carved heads of the retinue of Guru Rinpoche are worn by monk actors who move slowly downstage to sit on low thrones. Their colleagues shade them with large parasols. When the Guru Rinpoche figure appears, victorious over the eighth-century forces of recalcitrant landowners, jealous gods, and demons, a great silence falls over the crowd. People begin to prostrate, and everyone remains with hands in *anjali*, prayer position, while Guru Rinpoche takes his throne seat. At that point the pageant itself concludes and a procession of lay people is formed, starting with the VIP tent. One by one, they make offerings of white scarves, food, and money, first to Guru Rinpoche, and then to each of the characters in the retinue.

The magic of the afternoon runs through me. The spirit of the dances and the spirit of the Tibetan *sangha*, circulate like water or blood in my body. But I am exhausted by sun and crowds and iconography, and I retreat to the guest house, in a courtyard in back of the monastery. I lie down on the narrow

122

bed in my room, listen to the buzz of the dispersing crowd, close my eyes and in my mind's eye I see the great smiling face of His Holiness, Dilgo Khyentse Rinpoche.

March 29

Something came over me last night, like a slow dance in a dream. I kept getting up, shaken awake by images of Thrangu Rinpoche giving me a message, and then I'd go to the bathroom and empty my bowels. By this morning I realize it's dysentery. I don't feel wretched, simply weak and disoriented. What kind messages created this dreamy, disturbing dance all night.

I skip breakfast and morning meditation and go across the main road with a stool sample in a plastic film canister to wait for the doctor at the New Boudha Pharmacy. I've been through the system before, that's comforting, but the line in the modest cement waiting room is full—mostly parents with small children. Watching the children move around trying to amuse themselves takes most of my attention. I'm continually amazed by their natural flexibility and the details of their fine features. Observing the tenderness and propriety between parents and children reminds me that infant mortality is still high, but if a child survives to the age of five, her chance to live increases considerably. Still, not many Nepalese families can routinely visit a clinic doctor because of the fee.

The doctor arrives still wearing his motor scooter helmet and all eyes follow him to the door of his office. When it's my turn, in our three minute transaction, he acknowledges me from three years ago as he hands me my receipt. I've noticed before how people in official positions are often very simple and business-like. Late this afternoon or tomorrow, I'll get the lab results. When I report back to Wendell, we speculate on the source of the bacteria. We figure it's the new lunch place we tried out these last two days which had seemed so promising. Knowing he'll probably be next, we discuss the routine and the options.

After the seminar, we go to visit the five year old incarnation of Khyentse Rinpoche at the monastery of his uncle, Chokyi Nyima Rinpoche. The official announcement of his discovery came just after I left Nepal in December of '95, but even before that, rumors were circulating. I've been anxious to see him, and a little hesitant since I don't have the same connection to Chokyi Nyima's monastery that I have to Pullihari Monastery.

We are ushered into a large room where the young boy sits high up on an unembellished throne that looks more like a

work station. He is singing, *"Mary had a little lamb, little lamb,
little lamb..."* and when he comes to the last line, he makes up
the words in a phonetic combination that sounds like English
but is incomprehensible. He looks at me, so I say, *"her fleece was
white as snow."* His expression is inscrutable. I'm uncertain if it's
neutral or slightly mocking. The next time he sings, he pauses
at the same line and I take it as a cue and repeat, *"her fleece was
white as snow."* His expression seems to harden. When he
repeats his incomprehensible phonetic version, I regret my
boldness altogether. There is a moment of silence, and then
he points at me and says, *"You can go now."* My heart sinks. I
feel like a fool. As we bow and retreat towards the door, he
sing-songs, *"bye-bye, bye-bye, bye-bye."*

Outside in the hallway where we've left our shoes, I
glance at Wendell and we have the same dazed look, as if to
say, *"What was that about?"* Before we can exchange words, a well-
dressed Tibetan man, another visitor, hands me a business card
for his packing and shipping company and encourages me to
stop by and see him. I mumble something about having already
shipped everything. The fabrication is unintentional.

Later I describe our meeting with the Khyenste *yangsi* as
he is called, to an American nun who lives at Sechen Monastery. In a matter of fact way, she tells me that he has said this

125

to her with the same intonation, on several occasions. It certainly gives the visitor a clear direction in a situation that can be mesmerizing. I remember encountering the previous Khyentse Rinpoche several times and being utterly speechless. The first time I saw him, I entered a room by the wrong door and came face to face with the giant presence of the man seated on a throne of brocade and silk. My mind stopped short and for a brief moment I forgot where I was or why I'd come there. Spaciousness—at once timeless and extended present time—is the hallmark of the experience of meeting an enlightened teacher. Similarly, a strong moment of uncertainty, where one almost loses one's bearings, creates a comparable effect. *"You can go now."*

March 30

This is the last week of the Mahamudra seminar. The days have gotten busy with preparations for our journey to the Langtang district, the sacred valley of Yolmo, as it's known to Tibetans. The valley is one of four sacred valleys that Guru Rinpoche predicted would be places of refuge for Tibetan Buddhists at a time when harm would come to Tibet. And in fact, since the Chinese invasion of Tibet, strong dharma centers have developed in these valleys.

The seminar teachings seem more and more precious these last few days and the atmosphere of the shrine room with all the students and monks sitting there has stilled and settled. We feel like a family, almost like part of the monastery. There's the man who sits next to me every day and has never said a word. There's a woman who always comes in late and squeezes in front of me, then apologizes, asking if she's blocking my view. And a fellow with a taut physique and expression who wears short shorts and a sleeveless shirt, carries his bicycle helmet, a notepad and special cushion, and continuously writes notes, never looking up. And people whose names I now know and where they come from and how long they are here. And me, with my water bottle, French notebook and Indian shawl.

Several people have shaven their heads and taken monastic robes this last week. When I ask about that, I'm told that while Westerners are not encouraged to do this, they can receive monastic precepts and wear robes for a trial period.

By this time, Thrangu Rinpoche is a warm and familiar presence in the room. He speaks in Tibetan which is then translated. One has ample time to gaze up at him during the Tibetan section, before taking notes during the translation. His teaching style is absolutely straightforward and his response to questions exceedingly patient yet direct. I sense that he intuits the level of understanding of the student and responds accordingly.

Thrangu Rinpoche's smile is more like a feature of his face than an expression and has public forms including beaming and grinning. In private I've noticed another smile, even gentler, more inward. He is available for personal interviews nearly every afternoon and these are conducted without a translator in his sitting room, which feels cozy and quite ordinary. I'd arrived at my first interview almost breathless. It was my third day here and I had miscalculated the time it would take to get from one place to another. I was anxious and I had no time to collect myself. When I entered the sitting room all those concerns emptied out so suddenly I thought I was getting dizzy, wondered where I'd come from. The immediate past dropped away and the present was so spacious.

From a tent set up at the Stupa for the third day in a row, loudspeakers blare out information. A festival of some kind is coming up and while yesterday it sounded like recitation of prayers, today it has the tone of a war-time news report. The other report—from the lab—was negative, but it's certain both Wendell and I have dysentery. At the seminar this morning, we talked to an American nurse who works at the Embassy and now we're taking an antibiotic called Norbactin and eating noodle soup—*thukpa*—twice a day.

I find myself more sensitive during this condition and the crowds, the pollution and the noise of the loudspeakers is almost intolerable. I go inside a friend's shop to sit down in the back and recover. He brings me lemon tea and I rest for a while and watch the eight year old boy who sits every morning on a woven rope stool in front of the Goodwill Handicrafts Center. With his pink plastic sandals on the ground and his legs crossed under him, he looks like a little prince, perusing his illustrated book and playing with his Star Wars wristwatch.

When my energy returns, I have some dealings with the Indian tailor, who sits like a pasha on a wide cushioned bench which runs the length of his narrow fabric shop. With the help of two assistants he does business without ever getting up. Most of the bolts of fabric are in cubby holes above him, so he can scoot around and reach for them. I recently noticed that his leg is lame, but he is also so heavy, I assume it's inconvenient to get down from the cushions and stand on the floor.

He's as sharp as any merchant in the neighborhood. His eyes flash at every turn in the conversation. Bargaining with him is hopeless, so unless you want to go downtown, you make the best of it—his brocades are the finest local collection. Brocades are made in India, particularly in Benares, so they are a luxury item in Nepal. With all the monasteries around, his shop does a brisk business.

He and I have come to reasonable terms in my last few transactions, but I still enter his shop like an undercover agent on a mission. I have to simulate surprise at certain prices, shake my head, express disappointment or else I'm not doing my part to keep him honest. Now he apologizes for a misunderstanding we've had about the price per meter. I'd assumed we were negotiating meters but he informs me that with brocade, it's a "Benares square," a twenty-five percent size and cost difference. I'm truly miffed and while he is implacable, it's easy for me to act out the disappointment, head shaking, pouting and so on. In the end, I know he's been honest enough when he comes down nearly ten percent on the final price.

When I leave I carry the intensity of doing business with him for about a dozen steps outside before I remember that it was all a game to begin with. I almost believed that I was truly upset, but at this moment I see right through it. I laugh out loud when that happens and then I run into Ani-la who is on her way into the shop, and by the grin on my face, she seems to know exactly what has transpired. We go next door to Three Sisters Restaurant for a banana *lassi*, her favorite yogurt drink, and I ask her to describe her transactions with the fabric pasha. I like to check my experiences with Ani-la not only because she knows her way around, but because she's so efficient that she can run a household and accomplish the work of a full staff by herself. With a big smile she says, "*Yes, fabric buying, Indian way.*"

March 31

Today is a special Tamangi holiday which will be celebrated at the Great Stupa of Dharmakaya and then at the Swayambunath Stupa. Tamangs are a sizeable Tibeto-Nepalese ethnic group from the eastern hills surrounding the Kathmandu Valley. It turns out that this multi-day celebration is what the tent and loudspeakers are about—people will eat, drink, and dance all day and night and sleep at the Stupa. Then they will move on to the Swayambunath Stupa. What I hear about the celebration is just snippets. This particular holiday is such an auspicious time that Tamangi women come here to give birth and young people come to seek marriage partners. I've heard that a man can approach any woman he wants. I've also heard that they will exchange insults and if the man gets the last word, he can marry her. If the woman gets the last word, she can refuse. This is how it's told to me. I wonder who officiates, and who allows whom to get the last word.

I've introduced Wendell to a barbershop routine I used to have here and with his added enthusiasm, we frequent one place regularly. The shop is a cubicle on one of the streets that leads from behind the Stupa up into the hills. It's in a row of similar cubicles which sell Buddhist religious items, fruits and vegetables, soft drinks, fried lunch foods; cubicles that repeat themselves on all these streets.

The barbershop is about six feet wide by ten feet long, with Bugs Bunny and Elmer Fudd curtains for front doors, and four barber stations inside. Each station has a counter with a drawer underneath holding straight-edge razors, combs and a mirror above. On the counter are shaving cream and brushes, a cup for water, and the after-shave appointments. There are four different applications for the face which occur in this order: an astringent soap, toilet water, cream from a tube, and a transparent rock shaped object that cools when rubbed on the skin. Three or four neatly dressed young men work inside at any time. There is no apparent management, so prices vary from day to day, depending on who works on you or what you negotiate beforehand.

A typical shave goes like this: five minutes of face lathering, a kind of slow introduction in two stages separated by a pause, where the barber takes in the room and the other customers and changes the razor blade. The fresh blade is encouraging because the shop is orderly but not clean. Although I came through my initial phobia three years ago, the condition of the instruments, cloths, and towels keeps many foreigners away.

As the barber begins, he wipes the used lather onto the back of his hand. When his hand is full, he scrapes it off with the razor onto a piece of newsprint, taking one from the stack of small squares on the counter. He moves and works with grace and attention and a light, reassuring touch of his fingertips. After the four rubbing applications the shave is complete and the massage begins.

133

If you don't know about the massage, it's too late by the time he gets underway. Not until ten or fifteen minutes into the massage does he ask whether you want the full torso or just the standard head and shoulders. Of course he doesn't really ask in English, you just figure it out the first time. Gradually, you learn what to ask for before you sit down in the chair. I always say it twice, both times indicating with gestures, because the full massage can take up to forty minutes and leave you slightly delirious.

The more I go there, the closer I get to understanding that I can ask for, and sometimes get, exactly what I want. For example, before the first step in the massage process, he sprays your head and face with cold water from a Coke bottle. Naturally, the temperature of the water is a shock, but I'm also paranoid about untreated water near my mouth since a drop of it can induce *giardia*, the dreaded intestinal tract amoeba. So I've learned to hold up my hand and stop him each time he lifts the Coke bottle. In the same way, I can eliminate the hair gel at the end. I put my bag or an extra shirt over the towel he places on the counter for me to rest my face while he works on my spine. The towel is not too dirty, but it's already been used to wipe every customer's face, including mine. I haven't yet figured out a way around that.

He begins the actual massage by rubbing my scalp, drumming it. Then he moves down the spine, pummeling and probing. Today I beseech him. *"Gently please,"* I say, holding my stomach, which is still cramped from antibiotics. He interprets gently as slowly, which is actually quite nice and amounts to the same thing. Every so often he looks at me and says, *"Good? Slowly."*

The next stage of the massage is spinal twists, where he positions and levers himself so he can manipulate my whole spine. I am at least fifty per cent larger than he is and while his efforts rarely produce an adjustment, his intention gives me a good feeling. The final part is a series where he pulls and twists upper and lower arms, fingers, and neck—not for the faint of heart. As far as I know, barbers are a caste, trained in working the whole body as well as the face and head. Like every Nepalese worker their wages are poor. That's confirmed by the look in the barber's eyes when I give him a ten rupee tip in addition to the fifty rupee, or seventy-five cent shave and massage. He bows and I am so grateful that at the moment, I want to set him up, sponsor him in business.

I love and dread the barbershop. We've become regulars in here and one or two barbers in particular like to work on us meaty Americans. Teenage boys come through the Disney curtains to wet and comb their hair in front of the mirror. They enter and exit in a continuous stream, picking the comb up off the counter and putting it back down. Nobody objects to their primping. I imagine that they don't have mirrors of their own, or else it's too dark inside their rooms.

Younger kids enter the shop and stand near the chairs or in the corners just to observe the operations. They are delighted by the display. Everybody enjoys the crazy wallpaper of Hindu gods pasted up next to Hindu movie stars, all cut out from magazines and equally faded, peeling and mildewed. And everybody likes the film music blaring from a fractured cassette player in the corner, covered in a coat of hair clippings.

April 1

We finally got to Pashupati, the holiest Hindu section of Kathmandu, along the Bagmati River. On our walk there we accidentally came across the Naropa and Tilopa caves I'd been told about. In Boudha, while a friend was describing how to get there, I'd stopped listening to the instructions because they were too complicated. The only reason we found the caves was because I led us down the stairs onto the wrong side of the Bagmati River and we wound up inside the Golden

Temple compound, the grounds *"Forbidden To Non-Hindus."* As we landed there, a few people rushed at us, including a guard with a stick, pointing to the *"Forbidden"* sign and shouting. We held up our hands and hunched our shoulders in submission. As we retreated, I suppressed a grin because it suddenly felt like an action movie, the "angry mobs" and all.

Retracing our way down another set of stairs to the river, we found the caves. Although they are sealed and the names Naropa and Tilopa are garishly printed in red paint, I have a sense of devotion just looking at the caves and recalling the lineage of yogi saints who meditated in caves here and else-where throught the continent. Tilopa is the master whom Naropa finally meets after much searching and twelve years of specific trials.

Meditating in caves is a practice that is still very alive in Tibetan Buddhism. In fact the destination of our journey to Yolmo is a Guru Rinpoche cave in the Langtang region where we will practice meditation and receive teachings from Thrangu Rinpoche. Now, sitting cross-legged in front of the caves of pre-eminent masters of the Kagyu lineage, chanting the supplication to this lineage, I try to envision the week we will spend sitting like this high up in the sacred mountain valley cave of Guru Rinpoche.

While we sit, a pair of small spotted dogs appears in front of a shack built into the rock walls. They are followed by a beautiful woman carrying a basket and as they cross the river I sense their connection to this sacred place, as if they were consort and companions to Naropa himself.

There are spots in the Kathmandu Valley where one can sit for some time while the power of the place is revealed. It's an ordinary way of perceiving and feeling heightened by the attention one offers to the surroundings. Quieting one's chattering mind while extending one's sense perceptions out to the environment marks the beginning of this offering.

When we cross the nearly dry river bed on a bridge of sand bags and enter the heart of Pashupati, I remember that this whole area holds that power of place. Keith Dowman, a British writer and scholar who has lived and studied in Kathmandu since the early 1970s, and first guided me through Pashupati, elucidates this in his book, *Power Places in Kathmandu*. By the time we get to the cremation ghats along the river, we are prepared to sit and wait as the afternoon unfolds. Relaxing like this further awakens perception.

Above the river, from a series of terraced stone steps, I watch a sweeper move from one spot to another. Barefoot, dressed in thin white cottons, he carries his broom and leans against one wall, then another. He too is watching. People come to a well pump carrying plastic buckets, or simply hold out a cupped hand to drink as they prime the pump with the other hand. In the same way, others wash their feet and face. Their movements are delicate. Their loose clothing spreads out in folds around them.

Across the river a corpse wrapped in a saffron and red bedspread lies on a narrow step covered with yellow garlands of flowers. A man sits next to it, smoking a cigarette. The family of the deceased waits in the background. After dark we watch the cremation fire on the burning *ghat* further down the river. The *ghats* are arranged in caste order: Brahmin-priests, *Chetri*-warriors, then business caste, then untouch-ables. On the other side of the bridge are *ghats* for special people. And on our side of the river is a low *ghat* for foreign-ers who die here.

A friend from New York has drawn a map to a cluster of houses where five years ago she witnessed and photographed a coming of age ceremony for nine to eleven year old boys. She'd been invited in for the traditional feast after the head shaving and rituals ended and for years she's carried these images in a series of photos which she's asked me to give to the families. I can't believe I will ever find the place, but armed with the photos, it's easy detective work among the neighbors.

We are shown to a small house in the center of a tightly clustered compound of dwellings where a woman comes forward, studies the first few images, then squeals and beams at the sight of her younger brothers and parents. Immediately, relatives and neighbors crowd around the snapshots picking out familiar faces. When the excitement dies down, the woman escorts us into the front room of her house—a dark, two room brick structure—and seats us on a daybed. It's musty and close, so when she offers food and drink I decline by asking if we can sit outside.

By the time we negotiate that move and get to their tiny garden in back, her husband has arrived. His English is good and he replaces his six year old son as our go between in conversation. Although I learn facts and details of their lives— they own the house, the roof is unfinished so they can build a second story when they have more money, the wife earns money from sewing and weaving—the man is not so inter- ested in the photos as he is in telling us about his employ- ment situation. He worked at a large downtown hotel, then trained staff at a new hotel and was fired afterwards. He went to Saudi Arabia on a two year contract which didn't work out, and now he is unemployed. As he goes on, I long for the fragments of conversation we were having with his clever six year old son, which left a lot to my imagination. I regret that the wife now slips into the background as I sense the conversation leading towards the inevitable test of how we might participate in helping this man. And though I'm curious about the meeting itself and the exchange of the photographs, what is imperceptibly building here saddens me. I've been leaned on like this so many times. Because this family is middle class, I hadn't expected it to turn out this way. The man now wants to show us around the city in the days to come, and I am grateful I've been through this before and can dismiss the offer in a simple way.

April 2

It is morning. I'm in bed, eyes still closed, naming the discrete sounds of the street: carpet washing, thumping, sandals scuffing, distant radio, women's voices trailing by, then rooster, dove, bicycle bell. Soon the potato *wallah* will come by and I'll get up.

Yesterday was the last day of the seminar and in the closing ceremony, everyone was tearful as Thrangu Rinpoche

141

offered each of us small gifts and thanked us for traveling long distances and taking on financial hardships to come and study the dharma. Out in the courtyard during their lunch break, the little monks are running around as usual, eating cookies, shouting, playing tag.

In the newspaper today, NATO air strikes on Yugoslavia continue and Nepal seems like a sanctuary from ethnic cleansing. Israeli girls light Passover candles at their embassy downtown, and I note that it's another grand concurrence of special days: April Fools', Good Friday, Passover, full moon. It could very well be a Nepali holiday as well—there are more than a hundred of them in a given year.

I have two tailoring missions to accomplish before we leave on our trek tomorrow. Neither one seems complicated, but I know better and suspect they will consume much of the day. The first is to get downtown to "*Your Ravindra Tailoring*," a tortuous taxi ride because it is deep inside the downtown shopping district. I've given Mr. Ravindra models of jacket, pants, shirts and vests to duplicate, and brought him all the fabric, measured out. Most of the fabric comes from India. It's ironic that Indian tailors are unimpressive while the Nepalese can copy patterns and samples so skillfully. Today is the big fitting so that the clothes can be ready when we return from the Yolmo trek and retreat. I keep telling myself it's all worth it because I constantly wear the clothes I had made last time I was here. Anyway, the whole process appeals to my old world sensibility—where else could I afford to have clothes custom made?

I'm nauseous from the taxi ride by the time I get in the door, and I excuse myself to go down to the squatting toilet and then out to the street again for a bottle of water. Typically, nobody pays attention to one's condition. In this case that's an advantage since it helps me ignore how poorly I feel.

The first time I came here, I admired the workmanship of suits and shirts hanging in the shop as well as the odd, old sign on the door, *"Everest Dairy."* The shop has a good feeling to it, a flavor of downtown Kathmandu professionalism. And though the men squat and sit on the floor in front of fifty year old treadle machines, the scene is familiar to me. Maybe it's because my family photo album showcases my grandmother's seven sisters, all of them immigrant seamstresses in New York City in the 1920s.

Mr. Ravindra keeps his accounts in a crammed school ledger and writes measurements on a large scrap of brown paper. The jacket and pants I've given him as models are vintage forties and he balks at some of the unusual details. He wants to make it more modern, which in Nepal will bring us into the sixties. We discuss and consider the options and in the end I hold firm. He agrees and we shake hands.

I continue back to Boudha and on to Padma Tailors in one of the street cubicles. I walk past this shop every day and what finally catches my eye is a display of tall ceremonial bamboo arrows. While looking them over, I observe the way the shopkeeper talks to his customers. I make a mental note to try him out with something and last week the perfect opportunity arose. I volunteered to have text covers made for the retreat, a total of eighteen maroon cloth covers fitted to the size of the text we will use for the meditation practice in the Guru Rinpoche cave. The owner and I measure and design them together, consulting with the tailor.

Three days ago I came by to check on the progress and the one that had been finished was too small. After another consultation, production resumed. Now I've been checking back twice a day and this morning, although only a few were done, he kept promising. This afternoon, before I left for "*Your Ravindra Tailoring,*" he told me a few more were finished but the tailor was gone for lunch. It was three, well past lunchtime, but the tailor lives in Kopan, a forty minute walk up into the foothills. On my return at seven in the evening, an hour past closing time, still not finished.

I tell him we are having a group dinner for the retreat in a restaurant across the main street, that we'll be there until nine. *"Yes, yes, we bring them."* At half past nine the group is lined up at the cashier's table, slowly paying the bill, one at a time, when up the stairs come the owner and the tailor with broad smiles and all the book covers under their arms. We are all pleased and everyone bows and shakes hands several times.

On the way home, in the dark, I cross paths with the tailor at the Stupa. He gestures towards the hills. He's starting home to Kopan. I think of the pilgrimage, our trek tomorrow into those hills and far beyond. The tailor and I stand for a moment looking at the night sky and then he carefully takes my hand in both of his and gently bows.

Map of "Guru Rinpoche Journey"

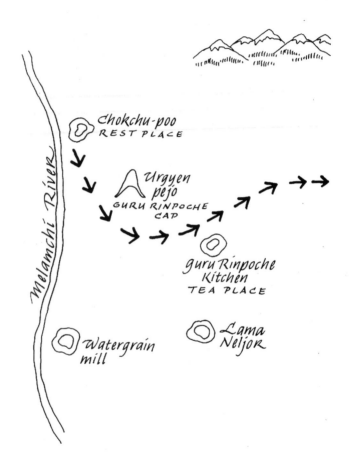

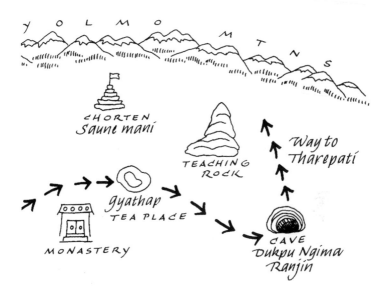

Y O L M O M T N S

CHORTEN
Saune mani

TEACHING
ROCK

Way to
Tharepati

gyathap
TEA PLACE

MONASTERY

CAVE
Dukpu Ngima
Ranjin

Khandoma Thara
WEAVING PLACE

CAVE
Zangbune

BATH PLACE

4

PILGRIMAGE TO YOLMO

While my body feels its age, my spirit grows younger in Nepal. I shed some psychological burdens and the remainder stand out in sharp relief. These old habits—conditions of self—as I know them, shift. I can't keep them going here in the usual way. At the same time, I can easily lose what bearings are left. It's a delicate state—something noticeably dropped away but not replaced—literally, lightened. Certain Buddhist slogans, like "regard all dharmas as dreams" and particularly, "whichever of the two occurs (losing what you have, not finding what you want), be patient" come alive here as if in these surroundings one resonates differently with them. All this runs through me as I sort out clothing, texts, equipment for the trek to Yolmo. Preparation also lives in the moment. How will I fare?

April 3

Today we leave for Yolmo in the Langtang Valley, northeast of Kathmandu. There's a pile of bags on the street, a pickup truck with the camping equipment, and a dozen kids milling around asking for money, soda, candy, pencils. Luggage seems to create a sensory attraction for street kids.

We are a large group, ranging in age from eighteen to sixty-six: the trekkers—lamas, nuns, and Westerners, seventeen in all; and the trekking crew of sherpas, cooks, and porters. It will take me a while to sort out and count the trekking crew, but six of them are sherpas, the guides who direct the operations, set up camp, serve tea and meals.

When everyone has gathered and the pickup is loaded, the porters carry the excess and we move onto the street, where a bus awaits. Amidst shouting and laughing and directives, the porters toss one piece at a time up onto the roof of the bus. When the pile is about four feet high, they tie it down and load the remainder into the back.

The rest of us mill around observing the goings on. I wonder if anyone has the same anxiety I do about fitting into the bus. I've often watched this procedure and reflected on the gap between their concept of a full vehicle and mine. For

Nepalese, a bus is full when every human, animal or object that wants to be on board, *is* on board. Room to sit, stand, or breathe properly is not a factor. Nor is the weight of passengers or cargo.

As I await the loading of humans, I prepare myself for the inevitable. Porters will stand in the aisles, sit on luggage in the rear and ride on the roof. And we, along with the sherpas, will take the regular seats, open the windows and cover our faces with dust masks and sunglasses. Then it's a question of just how hot, how many interminable stops for food, for water, oil, and gas, how many roadblocks for district custom inspections, and how many unsuspected wrong turns.

I think of trips taken in my life, and I consider my general wariness about traveling in large groups. I watch my mind work on this, chew on it, until on the bus, knees jammed into the seat in front of me, I'm distracted by a conversation with Dawa Sherpa, the young man sitting next to me. He's telling me about his home in Khumbu, the Everest region where sherpas come from and how he grew up the youngest and only boy in a family with six girls. He is so engaging. Although I know these exchanges can easily turn into requests for help, I freely play my part in the conversation.

The bus winds through high foothills surrounding the Kathmandu Valley, slowly grinding its way around sharp curve

153

after curve, past the ancient city state of Bhaktipur, up to Dhulikel with its dozens of tourist resorts, past the urban sprawl of Banepa, the first major bazaar town along the route. This road was built by the Chinese in the early 1960s. Before that, Banepa, twenty miles from Kathmandu, was a day's walk. Through dust and traffic, our loaded-down bus reaches here in ninety minutes.

As we move into more remote areas, the Indrawati River appears and splashes of green crops replace the landscape of dust-covered trees and wilting vegetation. The first rice terraces appear, above barley and wheat fields plowed by teams of yaks and oxen. Below us, egrets and kingfishers soar through small palm trees, skimming the surface of the water where sun-darkened children play and swim. The rushing Himalayan river calls out the beauty and sustenance of the land and its people, and, for the time being, loosens the remainder of my apprehension.

Hours later the bus lets us off at Melamchi Bazaar. The road continues for two more miles before it changes to the footpaths that meander up into the Langtang Valley. Melamchi Bazaar is like a wild west town of unfinished, run-down wooden and brick facades, cheap hotels, open stalls of merchandise, crumbling sidewalks, and the usual crowd of

154

kids reaching, pawing, asking for things. There's a disorder here, a sense of lawlessness, which continues through the next few towns as well.

We walk for three hours until shadows appear, then we pause in a one street town. Among us, only Yeshe, the British nun who has organized this pilgrimage, and one sherpa leader have been in this region before, and they consult some townspeople about a camping spot. By the time we set out again, it's nearly dark. The fifteen minute walk across small makeshift bridges of planks and rocks, and along sandy inlets, seems much longer in the dusk.

When we arrive at a large flat field set between two forks of the river, in the last evening light, the sherpas put up tents, the cooks set up the kitchen and the porters straggle in through darkness for the next hour. Before dinner is served, I'm asleep in the beautiful din of surging river water.

April 4

It is glorious to awaken to the sound of rapid waters and the call of river birds at dawn. Wendell and I talk together as we stay in our sleeping bags and assess the first twenty-four hours of the journey. The tent is cozy in the morning with soft luggage pushed against the side walls, shoes in front of the flap, and side windows unzipped. Dawa Sherpa announces tea and hands large stainless steel mugs through the tent flap. This is the traditional service offered by sherpas and this first morning it reminds me that even though the porters are out of sight much of the time, we are a whole camp here, more than fifty of us.

Within the first hour, we learn the traveling ropes—airing out and rolling up sleeping bags, packing up luggage, so the porters can set out ahead of us. It's a mystery how they know which trails to follow where no prescribed route exists. The routine for meals is fixed this morning when a large blue tarpaulin is spread out and places for the seventeen of us are set around it. One of the kitchen crew bangs a pot and we are called to the meal—nuns and monks from meditation and chanting, some of us from a quick bath at semi-private spots along the river, some from short strolls in the field. I've been photographing and writing about the trek's beginning.

All the gear is too much for the original crew. Six additional local porters were hired this morning when they showed up at the campsite, giving us a total of twenty-seven. Despite the size of the operation, we leave by 7:45 and walk through a small paradise of rice farms, gurgling feeder streams, and thatch roof stone houses built into the hillside. Irrigation hoses run long distances along the ground and are hung onto poles to travel up and down slopes. Where water is plentiful, agriculture can sustain people for much of the long growing year.

Schoolchildren with bookbags, traders with produce for markets, and men and women farmers carrying straw and cut grain pass us in both directions. Farm animals graze and drink, look up and move aside where the trail narrows. By 8:15 the sun is hot. Within an hour, heat is a force to contend with and we adopt various styles of keeping wet—dipping hats and scarves into water, squeezing them out, wearing them until the process can be repeated at the next stream or water pump.

After lunch, the terrain changes again as we climb up and down in the foothills above the valley. The river grows more distant and the sun grows stronger. Where the trail narrows around ridges, the sherpas attend to the less experienced, and to some of the slower hikers. The oldest of our group is the most experienced trekker. Yeshe, who has told us that she walks at a snail's pace (*"if I can do this, anyone can"*), is indefatigable.

Hiking in hot sun is not new to me but it's been many years since I've done it and I notice today that my body is not responding well. I feel weakened and though I drink pint after pint of water, I'm still dehydrated. Most of the group is having

When I stick my head through the tent flap in the muted dawn light, the vista of dark, steep slopes with wind blown pines resembles a Chinese scroll painting and I forget momentarily where I am. I can't remember whether I slept through the night or was up for most of it, whether I'm rested or uncomfortable. And who are these shadows moving around the tents, carrying tea kettles?

The morning proceeds with this sense of disorientation. Breakfast is late, lunch is early; the plan we made to leave later in the afternoon has dissolved and the sherpa leaders have us under way immediately after lunch. I linger over tying my boots, buying time to sort this out. We've got a four hour climb straight up and heading out at noon we'll hit the hottest part of the day for the entire way. I can't believe what is happening. I didn't do well in the sun yesterday, and I'm concerned about having enough water. Feeling like the sullen Boy Scout I sometimes was, I fall into line and we move single file down one wooded mountainside to the river, where the two thousand foot ascent up another mountainside to our destination begins.

The resistance I'm feeling thickens and nothing else exists. I'm trapped in it. A half hour later at the river, I imagine stopping, letting everyone else pass, and spending the afternoon swimming and lying in the shade. But I follow along, cross the suspension bridge and begin the first ascent which consists of about three hundred stone steps straight up, like a firefighter's extension ladder to the fifteenth floor. I climb quickly, thinking that if I exhaust myself, I might feel better. At the top there's pasture land, a small plateau where I find myself alone and start to feel almost normal again. But then one of the sherpas calls me back because I've gone off the trail. Again, I feel the resistance of being called back into line like a schoolboy.

This sudden, intense struggle with my state of mind shifts around like the clouds between the peaks overhead—darker to lighter to darker again. I piece together some lines from a Milarepa song we recited last night: *"There are no companions to tell you good news...when you want to remove sadness, there is no support. If you think, all sorts of meaningless thoughts will occur."* Of course it doesn't change anything but it does remind me that an enlightened being and great poet once struggled with his state of mind.

When I come to a stream and put my head into the rushing water, my mind momentarily clears—I look up and notice that the lamas and nuns have also stopped at the stream. They are drinking, soaking their handkerchiefs and they appear as unencumbered as the rushing water. When they start up again, I move in behind them. I'm too exhausted to keep up with my mind—my effort will be to simply follow the maroon robes of Lama Sherab and Lama Ajo.

For the next four hours, I climb in their company. I stop on the trail as Lama Sherab reads from a small local guide-book and points out landmarks and directions. From time to time, he recites prayers from another small book. I look where he and Lama Ajo look—at trees, at birds, at rock formations. When the whole group of monks and nuns rest, they seem to release their physical exertion as simply and thoroughly as removing their daypacks and setting them down.

The afternoon continues. I literally follow in their foot-steps, do as they do. I don't say much and that's a relief. I try the cubes of yak cheese which they suck on like rock candy. It tastes terrible. I spit it out.

Around one last bend after one last steep climb, the village of Melamchigyang comes into sight. It's the first real village we've seen in two days of walking. Yolmo or Helambu district is composed mainly of Tibetan Buddhist descendants. The population is considered Nepalese, but retains a regional dialect and Buddhist customs.

As I walk through the central courtyard of the village monastery and photograph in the glow of late afternoon light,

I see that the lamas are being invited into a tea garden, seated at a table with the village elder, and served butter tea. The nuns sit on the grass. When I wander over I am seated with the men and also served tea. I can tell that the elder is asking who I am. Older Tibetans are not shy—this old man looks directly at me and asks his question. Lama Sherab tells him that I am *"disciple."* The word sounds very grown up and committed, where I've been feeling like a child all day. I straighten my back and raise the cup to my lips. I can't stand butter tea, but determined to be a good disciple, I take a tentative sip. Evidently I made quite a grimace because the nuns start to giggle, point at me, and then double over with laughter. This sets the lhasa apsos barking and suddenly it's a full blown family comedy.

Just as suddenly, the sun sets and cool air sends chills through my sweat soaked shirt. I don't know where the cave is or how far we still have to go. The lamas' maroon robes look like the right attire and I picture myself huddling under their shawls.

It turns out to be only five minutes walk to the field where we are camping tonight. The tents are set up, the luggage is piled high, and a few of the group have already arrived. Wendell is sitting in front of our tent watching several children approach just close enough to glance at us, look us over. I join him and as we compare notes on the afternoon climb, I notice how at dusk, in this village of one hundred houses, I've slipped quietly into contentment.

April 6

At dawn the nuns sing morning prayers, sounding finger cymbals in accompaniment. A small dog scratches himself at our tent door. I recall the Milarepa feast practices we performed yesterday at the *Tiger Lion Fortress* cave. The lamas had a radiance about them as they led the ceremony, and later in the evening, they talked to each other animatedly, holding hands and laughing. They seemed delighted by this sacred spot.

I think about how I enfolded myself in their presence all afternoon, following their rhythm—walking and resting, listening and keeping silent. Another line from a Milarepa song comes to mind: *"Oh, what a pleasure it is to enjoy Confusion when as Wisdom it appears!"* Although I am struck by the sharp alternation of my emotions, I know from experience that emotion is heightened in retreat situations and that the contrasts are particularly strong at the beginning. Feelings just flare up then burn down, and one is left with embers, warming or smoldering.

163

The moon is still hanging over the tallest peak as I get a basin of water to wash myself. Our camp will move up to the ledge just below the cave itself, so it's another packing up morning. The nuns are busy cleaning the cave and setting up the shrine. Soon after breakfast, the sound of a distant helicopter alerts us that the arrival is earlier than expected. At once, the whole camp and the whole village is in motion. Everyone wants to be down in the field when the helicopter lands. From above, you can see villagers moving quickly down stone steps, carrying white scarves of offering and greeting. Schoolchildren are released from the school building and a group of five young men I met yesterday, who call themselves the "lay lamas" of the village, have gathered with horns and drums to form a musical procession.

I can't shift gears fast enough to join in the immediate movement, but in ten minutes, when the helicopter lands, I find myself flying down scores of stone steps, negotiating my way around slow moving old women and rushing with the crowd to the field. Rinpoche, his attendant Losang, and three Westerners who have accompanied him in the helicopter walk through the field. The lay lama band, impressive with purple shawls across their chests, leads the way. Most of the village adults either follow behind or line the trail from the village center up to the cave. Older women stand along the trail holding offerings of the homemade beer called *chang* and honey, both in bottles topped with yellow flowers.

Lama Ajo holds an umbrella over Thrangu Rinpoche to shield him from the sun while the other monks and nuns walk close by. The umbrella features a large orange and green 7-Eleven logos. The energy is vibrant. Faces in the crowd concentrate on Rinpoche, heads bowed, hands in prayer position. I've been told that the lama of the village recently died, a fact that makes Rinpoche's arrival all the more auspicious for the villagers. On the stone patio in front of the monastery, a few dozen schoolchildren in dark blue skirts and pants, light blue shirts and striped ties, line up as Rinpoche receives a *kata* from each of them and replaces it around their necks. Their school books, tied with a belt, hang at their sides.

As the entourage moves back onto the trail, I jump from rock to ledge to stone wall taking photographs. The procession moves slowly, but since the angles shift quickly as the path winds steadily uphill, I leap and sprint to keep a good vantage point. On the next to last ridge to the top, Lama Ajo, who is just in front of me, spots a water pump and peels off to get a drink, handing me the umbrella that he is holding over Rinpoche. I quickly shut down my lens, adjust the camera case across my chest, and take his place next to Rinpoche, guiding the umbrella up the steps and around bends. It's an honor to be in this position but it's a complex task, trying to coordinate the height and angle of the umbrella with Rinpoche's gait, his intermittent pauses, and the twisting steps.

When Rinpoche reaches the cave he goes directly inside. The villagers collect themselves in the outer courtyard and set their offerings down on a large flat rock. A chair is set up and when Rinpoche returns, he sits down and begins a blessing ceremony. One by one the villagers approach, the elder first, then all the rest of the men, then the older women, women with babies and small children, and a few children on their own. One boy stands transfixed in front of Rinpoche for a long time while the line progresses around him. Each person is given a laminated photo of Padmasambhava and a red string, a protection cord to tie around their neck.

The excitement of the crowd is evident. When the blessings are finished and Rinpoche has returned to his tent, people rush up to Lama Sonam, Rinpoche's cook, to get more photos and more protection cords. Meanwhile, the young men are pouring the homemade beer offerings into our hands and drinking it themselves. Lama Sonam is now surrounded by a beseeching mob. Unperturbed, even bemused, he hands out everything he has until there is nothing left to give.

After lunch, the energy settles down. Rinpoche's tent sits on a small ledge adjacent to the cave. It has bold blue dragons appliqueed to its roof. In the afternoon we begin the schedule. For the next five days we will recite texts and do meditation practice. Thrangu Rinpoche will teach on the text in the morning. In the afternoon, we will do a longer session, the full version of the text, and in the evening, after supper, there will be another devotional practice, led by the lamas and nuns.

This evening at supper, the cook, Ram, presents a cake inscribed with a welcome to Rinpoche. Although Rinpoche dines in his own tent, I sense his unifying presence among us all—Western students, monks, nuns, sherpas, villagers. Another larger tribe has temporarily come together—even the kitchen boys and the porters are beginning to relax and show themselves in a different way.

April 8

Yesterday was our first full practice day. *"Mantra"*—speech— the power of words and vocalization—is a part of meditation practice, meant to awaken one's senses as well as one's

167

physical and mental energies. The texts we chant and sing are rhythmic and melodic. The practice has a powerful effect—uplifting, cleansing, even celebratory. In two days' time, the cave has been transformed into a shrine room that welcomes and inspires a packed congregation of twenty-two people. Prayer (a word that Tibetans use easily where Western Buddhists like to say "practice") is appropriate here. It is alive in the meditation practice. It is equally alive in the daily life of Melamchigyang village. Because buddha nature, the seed of enlightenment, resides in every being, Tibetan Buddhist culture does not separate activity from prayer. Like spinning prayer wheels or circumambulating a stupa, daily life and daily prayer offering is ordinary and continuous.

The nuns are the keepers of the cave, shrine, and offerings. They have taken their places and blossomed. Their attention and composure are remarkable but it's their sense of humor and delight that thoroughly captures the group. At almost every meal now, one of the nuns or one of the Westerners will break up over some detail or story and provoke a contagious laughing fit. This morning it was my account of asking Dawa Sherpa about his expedition up the mountain. He's seen yaks grazing and tried to get yak butter. I think he says, "I *got hair-cut*." I look at him with self-interest in a possible nearby barber and admire his hair. "A *barber. Is there a village*?" "*No, only small house.*" "*Then how did you get haircut*?" Dawa pauses for a moment, then quietly and carefully, with a hint of a smile, says: "I *got yo-gut*."

Among ourselves in the mornings, there is extensive conversation about getting hot water for washing. Usually, trekking companies set up washing tents and prepare individual basins with hot water. But after four days of inquiries, it finally comes out that they forgot to bring the basins. We have taken matters into our own hands and tried different solutions. In the end, we've come up with a comedy of errors called, "*men washing day; women washing day.*" Of course it doesn't work. Not counting the monastics, there are now eleven women and only four men. The sherpas haven't the foggiest idea what we're up to. And in any case, there is a certain pleasure in chatting about it all whether it gets accomplished or not. Like our laughing fits, this relaxes the situation. It lightens our obsession with food, digestion, and the chances of getting a good night's sleep.

April 9

Opening the tent flap in the first light, I look out on the eastern peaks of the Yolmo mountains. The rock face is craggy and sparsely covered with firs. As the light changes during the day, its features shift. I have an ongoing discourse with the mountain in its various manifestations, like the one I have at home with the Shawangunk cliffs in the Hudson Valley. *Yol* means surrounding mountains and *mo* means woman. The mutable appearance of the range, the way it cradles the valley, underscores its feminine principle.

After gazing at the mountains, Wendell and I start our morning conversation, a kind of barely awake, stream of consciousness exchange that alternates between present, recent past in Nepal, and a shared historical past in New York. It turns easily to dharma these days now that we've been studying together for four weeks. This morning I speak about how neurosis, *klesha*, seems to rise up dramatically in retreat situations. It penetrates more directly here, where self-reference, self-aggression, is culturally weak. When I think, "*my* legs, *my* sleep, *my* washing," the contrast is stronger, more raw. I notice a slight revulsion at the depth of the most basic self-reference.

At the same time, the impact eases almost effortlessly, as though being aware of it creates a benevolent spirit into which it dissolves. I think about the line in the Kagyu lineage prayer we chant every morning, *"Revulsion is the foot of meditation."* The foot, the connection to the earth, the appendage that moves you along, one foot in front of the next.

This morning, the villagers filed up the steep path to the cave. The older women are barefoot. They carry woven Tibetan shoulder bags or Disney daypacks and wear long skirts and the traditional multi-colored striped woolen apron. They hold offerings and thermoses for the feast practice that Thrangu Rinpoche will perform for their deceased lama.

We have the morning off, and led by Yeshe and the nuns, some of us go off to explore a sacred rock outcropping on the mountainside to the west. It's known as the teaching rock because Guru Rinpoche is said to have given teachings there. This is the most dramatic of several places attributed to his activities, a long expanse of flat rock with a slab of boulder at one end that appears as a throne seat. As soon as we get there, the nuns begin to circumambulate the throne seat and prepare the materials for a smoke offering or *lhasang*. Dawa Sherpa and one of the porters scramble around collecting sticks and brush to start the fire, and juniper for the smoke.

171

Lhasang is a purification ceremony, an offering to a place, a situation or event. One either passes personal objects through the smoke of the fire offering to purify and empower them or simply waves the smoke onto one's body. In Trungpa Rinpoche's Shambhala community, we've used *lhasang* to mark beginnings—the commencement of meditation or community programs, the celebration of solstice and equinox, the construction of buildings, the consecration of sites.

We climb back down from the teaching rock and return to the village. Wendell and I wander to the field behind the monastery. It's school recess time. Older boys practice running high jump over a rope held by two younger ones. Little ones yell and run, giggling in games of tag and wrestling. Every school uniform is covered in dust. The high jump is compelling because of the boys' joy and concentration at play and the way they appreciate each other's achievement. Again I notice how the stillness to simply look and appreciate is strengthened, heightened by this retreat practice.

When recess is over, we follow the children back to the monastery which serves as classrooms until funds are raised to finish the school building. Sitting on a ledge watching girls and boys play games of checkers with pebbles, the village elder motions us to come and sit with him. Because his ten year old nephew is nearby and seems to speak enough English, I begin an impromptu interview with the old man. The translations keep fizzling out until a nearby lodge owner appears with a bound handmade book of the history of the village. From it, I copy out a map and whatever facts are written in numbers. Later, the village schoolteacher translates for me.

There are six castes, or family names in this village of 111 houses and 600 inhabitants. They are of Tibetan descent and speak a sherpa dialect of mixed Tibetan, Nepali and Tamangi. Half the families have left for seasonal work in India, where the women work in teahouses and on road crews along with boys and men. Apple orchards were a promising crop addition, but monkeys soon learned to gather all the fruit and eventually destroyed the trees. Trade in potatoes, radishes, garlic, onions and wheat goes only so far in exchange for rice and merchandise from the lower valley towns. Even in a well-organized and prosperous looking place like Melamchigyang, there is not enough to sustain the population.

April 10

During the afternoon practice session yesterday, it began to rain and quickly turned into an unstoppable downpour. Back in our tent I realize the rain is soaking through all the corners and forming a pool in the center. We shift everything around. Then we sit in our sleeping bags and wonder what will happen if more water gets in. We reflect on our experience up to this point. For the first time, I think of home, early spring flowers, and sleeping in my own bed. There is lightning, thunder, then the largest chunks of hail I've ever seen quickly cover the ground. How long can we hold out? I'm concerned about my clothes and notebooks getting soaked. Finally, the sherpas come to tell us that our tent and several others cannot withstand the storm. They will move us down to one of the lodges in the village. But first, while they carry our things down to the lodge, they say we *must* go up to the cave for dinner. I like their certainty here. I like the way they use the word *must*.

There's something in the emergency that calls out the best in the sherpas, as though they'd been waiting for this moment to spring into real action, beyond just setting up and taking down tents and serving tea. They are covered head to toe in yellow raingear and only their animated faces show through. On the way back from the cave, during a brief pause in the downpour, Dawa Sherpa regales us with the story of an avalanche on K3 in the Everest region where most of the group's climbing equipment was swept away. Walking down to the lodge, I see the other sherpas hanging out in the kitchen, drinking *rakshi*, the local brandy. These guys are prepared to save lives in an emergency. I can feel that energy moving now, their pleasure in taking charge.

The lodge belongs to the family of three children who were looking us over that first afternoon of arrival. And oddly, once we are installed in four separate rooms off a main foyer that serves as dining room and lounge, it's the children who take care of us. The elder boy, Tashi Dawa, helps his grandfather make a fire in the stove in the center of the room. His sister, Maya Tsering, gets the key to the supply cupboard so we can have water and toilet paper. And the younger boy, Phurba, scoots around offering advice and ideas about everything. He's the one who catches my attention. Though he says he's ten, and despite his wonderful grown-up outfit of gray corduroy pants, beige linen jacket with pointed lapels, and checked shirt buttoned to the top, he looks like a boy of six or seven. Like some of the others, under the tutelage of the excellent and dedicated young village teacher from Kathmandu who has taught here for fifteen years, Phurba's English is better than most Nepalese children. And unlike the shy approach I'm used to—questions about where I'm from, how I like Nepal—Phurba quickly, off-handedly engages me in a discussion about airplanes using a small, pocket model to illustrate his points. He was impressed with the helicopter landing and with the arrival of Thrangu Rinpoche, and he asks about both, contrasting the sounds and movement of a helicopter to that of an airplane, showing me the two red protection cords from the village blessing ceremony around his neck. As I move chairs close to the stove and drape my wet clothes over them, he examines my luggage, holds up my battery operated shaver and Swiss army knife for demonstration. I suddenly feel like I know him. He's the Little Prince. There is an airplane, an emergency, and I am Antoine de Saint-Exupery.

April 11

Through the great storm, while rain battered the corrugated tin roof, I slept peacefully and wake up curious and alert. The storm is over—at seven A.M. the sun is fully up. The children are occupied with chores—Phurba feeds the chickens, Maya Tsering washes last night's dishes, and Tashi Dawa draws water from the five hundred liter blue "*Polytank*."

Brushing my teeth out on the porch overlooking a garden patch of barley and potatoes I watch the big rooster move across to mount the hen. Chickens poke their heads through clusters of barley stalks. Baby lambs are bleating and hundreds of tall prayer flags around the village move gently in a small breeze. The air is clear. I turn to the mountains and witness the unexpected—fresh snow-covered peaks and the tallest among them—*Amma Yangri*—dakini goddess—sparkling like a fairytale maiden.

I've been sitting next to Lama Sherab and Lama Ajo at most meals. If I arrive after they do, they motion me to sit down next to them. I feel like the teacher's pet and I like it. Lama Sherab speaks some English, but both of them usually indicate when they communicate with me. So today I was surprised when Lama Sherab asked me how much a cup of coffee costs in the United States. It was odd to compose a simple answer, without getting involved in where you might be having that cup of coffee—New York City or a small town; at a hotel or at a luncheonette counter. But it was an excuse to ask him about his travels and about his plans. It was also the beginning of a personal dialogue with him.

Today, the Westerners are talking about departure dates and airline tickets. Most people will leave in a few days, just after we arrive back in Kathmandu. I have another week and even though I have been thinking of home, I'm not ready to go. I remember this about retreat practice. Just when you begin to feel the effect of settling down, you are pulled toward departure.

Before we began the trek, Yeshe told us of a saying that to practice for one day in Yolmo is the same as one year elsewhere. This morning I feel like I've been here for years, that in the moment, my awareness and appreciation has grown many times. There is certainly magic at work here. Part of that magic is that when my habitually fixed mind wears down, shifts to a slower speed, the world opens up and presents itself authentically, less overlaid by my projection, my opinion or evaluation. The gift of meditation practice, of retreat, is to experience the constant shifts that are natural to human existence without trying to control them. This is also the gift of living in a traditional Tibetan Buddhist culture.

April 12

The melodies of the puja practices sing themselves in my mind as I fall asleep and as I wake up. In the evening, the lamas and nuns do a practice called *"offering one's body,"* performed with large, hand held prayer drums and long thigh bone trumpets. The music and the vocal harmonies are haunting. I am content to sit and listen, gazing up at the wall of frescoes of Guru Rinpoche in four different emanations, grateful that my body has made it through another day. Between sitting cross-legged much of the day and sleeping on a mat on the ground, the stiffness of the morning is one of the trials of this camping retreat.

Several of the sherpas have been sitting in on the practice sessions. One of the sherpa leaders comes regularly now, sits with the lamas, shares a text and chants the prayers. It turns out that as a boy, he was a monk living in a monastery for twelve years. Monks are free to choose for themselves whether to stay or leave the monastery when they reach the age of eighteen. If they leave, they have at least gained a better education than public school. Yeshe tells us that up until now, the sherpa leader has been too shy to admit that he was a monk many years ago.

I sing one of the simple melodies to Phurba. He has been asking me for a photograph of Thrangu Rinpoche but I think the crowds got them all that first day. This morning he is interested only in the arrival of the helicopter which will take Rinpoche back to Kathmandu. *"Helicopter come. Helicopter come."* Each time Phurba repeats this I think he has actually heard sounds in the distance and I stop and listen. When I photograph him in front of one of the hand lettered signs on his family's Wildview Lodge Hotel: *Special for singale and double bed room. Hot and cold shower to bath. Local holley placese guide service*, I feel the deep connection I've made to this village.

Last night, after the final feast offering practice, Rinpoche ate dinner with us and a party was arranged. The whole village came up to receive blessings and partake in the feast food offerings. Once again Rinpoche blessed each one of them. It was poignant to observe the villagers, their faces now familiar to me, individually express their devotion.

In the evening the porters, kitchen staff, and sherpas were invited to sing and dance around a bonfire built on the large flat rock in the center of our dining courtyard. They carried on for about half an hour, most singing, a few dancing. Wendell and I were called out to dance with them and tried to simulate the simple traditional style of the men, waving arms and taking small folk dance steps, avoiding the sparks and smoke of the fire. Rinpoche enjoys dance and like other Tibetan teachers I've studied with, he invites his students to perform. I always find it unnerving when our Buddhist teachers ask us to perform. It challenges my notion of sacred and ordinary and directs my attention towards the offering itself.

As the Nepalese crew was running out of steam, Rinpoche left, and to keep the party going, the nuns encouraged the Westerners to sing. We floundered around at first, trying to find songs that both British and Americans had in common. Yeshe kept pushing Beatles songs, but since the Brits were too shy to give it much effort, it was up to the Americans. Once we got started, we couldn't stop. We went on and on, even after all the Nepalese had left, singing everything we knew—folk songs, old rock and roll ballads, show tunes. The nuns were delighted. Their satisfaction with vocalizing is unmistakable. Today at breakfast, they were still giggling and talking about it.

Rinpoche was doing one last ceremony for the deceased village lama in the field where four small stone cremation stupas stand. One of the stupas is covered in white ash, the sign of a recent cremation. At the sound of an approaching helicopter, all the children began running to the landing field.

Rinpoche finished the ceremony as the helicopter touched down and just as suddenly, it took off again, leaving everyone puzzled. Then we all sat in the field and waited. Rinpoche sat on a bench surrounded by the lamas and nuns, shaded by the big 7-Eleven umbrella. The older village men congregated in a corner of the field, the younger men grouped together elsewhere, women with small children sat in another corner, and older children played with stalks of tall grass and with pebbles.

There was a lot of speculation about the helicopter. Most likely it was a false landing by international field workers. In any case, we sat and sat, and to pass the time as the sun beat down, we gathered around Rinpoche—villagers and trekkers, separately and together, for an endless series of group portraits. By the time the helicopter finally arrived, we had settled into sitting around and literally passing the time of day. Being connected through Rinpoche had made the village feel like *sangha*, community. In the moments after the helicopter took off, there was a silence and a lull during which everyone simply stood in place, looking up at the chopper grow smaller in the sky.

April 13

Here we are back at *Takpuk Sengedzong*, Milarepa's Tiger Cave Lion Fortress. The attendant of the cave told the story of Milarepa's teacher, Marpa, trying to scare him by roaring like a tiger. Mila turned around and roared back like a lion, scaring Marpa. That was the last thing I remember before I went into my tent and slept for thirteen hours. I just passed out. When I woke this morning, I was alone, sprawled out in the tent, recovering from mild heatstroke. Wendell took the helicopter back to Kathmandu, so he would have two extras days. This last leg of the journey is already different without him.

14 April

Everybody feels familiar at this point. The descent is easier. Long, relaxed conversations ensue. A sherpa named Tshering is my guardian angel. He moves across the terrain like a mountain goat. Since witnessing my condition, he keeps within twenty feet of me all day. Because I'm feeling better, from time to time I try to lose him, but he is too persistent. Until now he's been quiet. His English is surprisingly good and when he opens up, he is more formal, professional, than the other young sherpas.

I observe Lama Sherab and Lama Ajo go off the trail to search for something and each time they return with bunches of herbs. This evening, after camp was set up in the same field of our first night out, surrounded by thundering streams, I sat with Lama Sherab and he asked me how I was feeling. His English is better than I suspected and we were able to communicate about heat fever. He gave me some of the wild ginger he and Lama Ajo had collected and started to explain how to cut and cook it. The instructions were unclear to me. Fortunately our translator sat down with us and the remedy was carefully repeated. Then I listened to her translation of Lama Sherab telling about his life. He studied Tibetan medicine with a practitioner in the district where he grew up. I had known that Lama Sherab is a Rinpoche who administrates several dozen monasteries and nunneries in Chum, a restricted area of Nepal on the Tibetan border. Listening to him talk about the practice of different Tibetan remedies, I am instantly drawn to the world of his native region, a place that remains much as it has always been. Given the opportunity I would walk with him to his land. That could be the next pilgrimage.

15 April

This last morning of the trek, everything appears to move in slow motion. I am carefully taking it in. I sort out what I want to give away to the staff and pack up the rest. Each thing seems precious—the last of the skin cream, the trusty pillow, the tee-shirt drying on river rocks, the field of maroon robes I've grown so used to.

We sit down to breakfast and suddenly a huge chocolate cake appears and we're singing "*Happy Birthday*" to David who is sixty years old this morning. Ram makes these cakes in a large circular tin, set into boiling water and covered with another tin. Sometimes they are as dense as brown bread, but this morning's breakfast chocolate cake is the best so far.

Then we take off, scrambling over river rocks. Everyone's gait seems lighter, every face brighter, as though we each shed unwanted burdens along this journey to Yolmo. The lamas have cut long sticks of thick bamboo, and carved the tips into ritual arrows which they carry wrapped in tufts of tall grass and tied to their daypacks. Yesterday, late in the afternoon, we saw a golden eagle and heard the arresting sound of cuckoos. This morning, passing farmers carrying huge loads of hay and women beating yucca to make rope, we re-enter the world of trade and markets.

185

My mind is busy with steps, busy with coming back from heat fever and so much sleep, and at the same time, drifting, releasing the energy of the retreat. I walk with Dawa Sherpa and talk about his future, his possibilities. I walk with Lama Ajo, keeping step as we point out things to each other naming words in Tibetan and English—a perfectly thatched roof over a small stone house; an egret on a bale of hay; a child splashing with a small dog in a mud puddle. I walk with schoolboys and ask them about their studies, their interests. They walk on both sides of me and their eager, lively energy is buoyant. My spirit has an abandon this morning, a wild expansiveness contained only by paying attention to the rhythm of walking and the rhythm of the surrounding life passing by me. I recognize this sheer joy as fruition and at the same time as path, as it literally is today. Milarepa sings, "*Looking no more for enlightenment, I am extremely happy. Free from both hope and fear, I feel very joyful.*"

When we stop along a wide stretch of the Indrawati River, minutes away from where the bus will meet us, we spread out along the stony bank while lunch is prepared. It's midday, the sun is scorching, but it's no match for the clear, rushing river water. I perch on a rock and watch Yeshe, in nun's robes, straw hat, and sunglasses, still holding her umbrella, submerge herself in the river.

186

A fisherman with a basket tied to his waist leaps from rock to rock moving downstream as he casts and re-casts a net weighted with small stones. Naked boys, with mud dried in light patches against their sun-blackened skin, dig up sod and practice being porters. Bent over, they carry the clumps of sod on their backs and carefully place them between river rocks, as though they were planting rice fields. Over and over, they repeat their movements until the rocks turn into an irregular mound of earth and grass.

Our porters squat in small plots of sand and receive their pay from one of the head sherpas. Then they wander off, some to bathe in the river, some in my direction, and I take a few last portraits. At lunch, one by one, the name of each staff member is read off and Lama Sherab presents each of them with a bonus from our group. It is poignant to watch them approach and receive the money. In one of the conversations I had this morning, we were talking about young men who tried to be porters and couldn't make it. At the age of twelve or fourteen, they'd be carrying these huge packs and weeping in pain and humiliation. I've witnessed two of our porters with twisted ankles, relieved of their loads, hobbling along with walking sticks. And over and over I've watched porters squat down while two men load the basket onto their back and then pull them up into standing position.

I experience sadness as the pitch of the retreat subsides and the prospect of a long dusty ride back to Kathmandu approaches. The ginger root remedy took the heat out of my body, but I woke up with a sore throat and a cold. So did Lama Ajo. I see him sniffling and his pace is slowed down.

It takes forever to load the bus. It's disconcerting to look at the worn down tires, the dragging axle, but the worst is yet to come. The seats have no springs and coupled with the absence of decent shock absorbers, the four hour ride is hellish. The subdued edginess among us is palpable. By the time we get to Kathmandu, I'm about to explode and even the British are ready to mutiny. It's so bad, it literally makes me laugh to watch myself get so close to losing it. Meanwhile, Ram, the cook, sitting next to me, has slept most of the way, his legs and slight frame bouncing against me while again and again I nudge him back to his side of the seat. We're like children on a long camping trip—one tired, grumpy bunch. And like children, we've taken a journey away from home and without yet knowing it, we've grown along the way.

I glance at Ram asleep at my side, unperturbed by these concerns. He must have been up very early this morning to make that chocolate cake.

189

5

LEAVING

It's not that time is fast or slow. Rather, perception deepens and less is taken for granted. Trungpa Rinpoche used to say, "Let the world come to you." When it does, life expands its ordinary boundaries; one lets go a layer of projection that normally intervenes and interprets. That slight decrease in projection is timely and appreciable. The world comes in and its details are more vivid. Feelings are sharper and the exchange more fluid. What reverberates for me is the Buddhist view that it is rare and precious to be born human, and even more so, to meet a realized teacher and to practice the Dharma.

April 16

Returning from a retreat always feels like re-entering another orbit. It was no different yesterday evening, stronger even after three days walking back from the Guru Rinpoche cave. The Boudha neighborhood seemed quite ordinary. I found my way to a friend's house for dinner. Today she commented that I followed her around from room to room like a puppy. I noticed that it was difficult to arrange consecutive logical sentences. Everything in the house was so bright and evocative, I kept getting lost in simple details of perception.

This is Wendell's last day before departure. Since he's got his affairs in order, he accompanies me for the first time to *Your Ravindra Tailoring* to pick up the custom made clothing. Two men are working in tandem on the buttonholes of a vest—the last detail to be finished. Mr. Ravindra orders tea for us and when the tea boy arrives, we are in the midst of trying on shirts and pants. It all works. The tailoring is impeccable. The men pause at their machines to admire the clothes and I joke with Mr. Ravindra about the vintage styling of the jacket.

This feels like the fruition stage of the journey. The trek to the cave and the retreat itself challenged my own concept of physical and mental well-being. I feel processed, changed by its rugged simplicity.

The limitations in a retreat situation are provocative, yet the simplicity brings out the distinct experience of freedom. The texture of this freedom is surprisingly clear and not separate from moment to moment awareness.

Another line from the Kagyu lineage chant says, "*Awareness is the body of meditation as is taught. Whatever arises is fresh, the nature of realization.*" I think of the poet Charles Olson's description of life being informed by and from one's body. The wisdom of one's knowing body has been neglected in modern society, where speed and competition cut off a vast amount of somatic information. Awareness brings us back; as practice, it joins mind and body. Life is informed by awareness, and awareness brings us home to our own true nature.

April 17

Taking Wendell to the airport is not a casual excursion. Although it requires a shorter and easier drive than going downtown, the airport is a singular institution, a piece of land that represents the boundary between Nepal and elsewhere.

193

Inside Tribuvan Airport one returns to a majority of foreigners, tourists. My orientation shifts to being an international traveler. The sense of the outside world is still elusive in Nepal. Foreigners only came here in significant numbers in the 1960's and the country still resonates with its own traditions more than it does with the rest of Asia or the international community.

We are surrounded by trolleys of luggage and stories of travel. We wait on line and listen to the family in front of us. The young man has married a Nepalese woman while serving in the Peace Corps, and his mother and sister have come from Michigan to visit for the first time. In another story, a young woman lost her backpack on a whitewater rafting expedition, and a guide was injured trying to retrieve it.

I think about the stories we are taking home, how they are never easy to articulate. I sense Wendell's energy shift towards home and feel mine holding out, waiting. This is a preview for my departure in five days. After getting through two long lines, we are free to have a cup of tea upstairs in the international lounge. There's not much left to say. I ask the waiter to take our picture beneath a blow-up of a potter at work. Moments later, I'm alone in a taxi driving back to Boudha.

April 21

The past few days have been consumed by local shopping errands and seeing friends. People here don't express sadness or regret at departures. In fact the parting gesture is similar to arrival—an offering scarf, *kata*, placed around one's neck.

Ani-la invites me to one last lunch and serves Bhutanese specialties—a cuisine she is known for among her friends—cellophane noodles with shredded beef, pink rice, sauteed peppers, potato salad. Ani-la is younger than I am but I have the same feeling of well-being in her kitchen that I used to have in my grandmother's—the feeling of being cared for without conditions.

I have an interview with Thrangu Rinpoche and as I'm leaving, my eyes fill with tears. Rinpoche reaches behind a shelf and hands me a pink tissue. The simple and complete gesture makes me smile. Again, no conditions, just offering. On my way out of the monastery I pause for a moment on a landing and Rinpoche's attendant Losang hurries up to me with a handful of photographs and pins. *"This is for you. Rinpoche would like you to come to dinner this evening. Can you come?"*

Dinner is again in the sitting room and very ordinary. We talk about things that are happening in the world and in the Buddhist community. Light fades in the sky with a dramatic darkening of clouds. I tell Rinpoche about my work and ask about his travels. Losang comes and goes with soup and rice, broccoli and chicken, ice cream and cookies and fruit. The electricity goes on and off a few times and at one point, we sit in candlelight. Rinpoche doesn't look or act any differently. The edge is all mine, alternating between simple awareness and a gap of *what next?* As I stand to leave, Losang brings out a thangka as a gift from Rinpoche. I ask him to unroll it. It's an unfinished, primitively painted Shakyamuni Buddha. Its simplicity is quite a contrast to the ornate and complex images one usually sees in thangkas. Accepting the gift, I bow to Rinpoche. *"This afternoon when I left, you gave me a tissue. Tonight, a thangka. What do you think it means?"* Rinpoche's grin breaks into laughter and I exit laughing.

April 22

My last errand is to pick up my hiking boots from the shoe repair man who sets up outside Thrangu Rinpoche's monastery, at a crossroads that I call "shishkebob junction" because of

the smoke and smell from skewers of meat sizzling at an open
grill morning until night. After I collect my boots, the man
gestures to ask if he can polish the shoes I'm wearing. Usually
there's no point to having your shoes shined because of the
dirt paths, but today I'm leaving and it seems fitting to take
this piece of Kathmandu street life with me. I sit down on a
wooden box that he's set up for customers and watch him mix
mustard seed powder with a reddish liquid then grind it into a
paste. The dust from dogs and pedestrians kicks up and the
smoke of the grill floats by. I fan away flies with a letter a monk
has given me to mail in the States. People stop to observe the
shoe polishing and I watch them watching us until I glance at
my shoes and notice that they've changed from tan to orange.
The shoe repair man seems pleased with the way it's going.
He's absorbed in deepening the color. I'm horrified at the
prospect of wearing orange shoes and indicate to him that the
color is too bright. Though he seems offended he is able to
tone it down. As the smoke blows over us, I imagine my shoes
as chickens roasting on a spit.

Meanwhile, a young man stands nearby, his face
smudged with black soot, applied like war paint. He beats his
bare chest while shouting staccato chants. Then he sings a
mournful melody. His emotions alternate from terrorizing cries

to pitiful moans. Watching him, I remember the dancing woman and the deranged boy from last month. Yesterday I saw the boy in the Three Sisters Restaurant accompanied by a European man. He was dressed in clean clothes and was eating with a fork. The man was talking to him and the boy was looking up in response.

I found out later that this man is a visiting massage therapist who made contact with the boy and brought him back into the world, at least for the time being. The Great Stupa of Dharmakaya is like an open air temple of sanity that seems to attract and accommodate all variety of disturbance as well as worship as part of its celebration of buddha nature.

Walking back to the guest house in my dayglo shoes, I meet Ani-la carrying a few last things for me to bring back to friends of hers in New York. I've got only thirty minutes left before leaving for the airport, but I feel unusually relaxed. A monk I've been trying to find for five days is waiting for me inside the guest house. I introduce the monk and the nun as I would any friends of mine, though the humor of the situation prevails. The monk, Oser, has brought some presents— beautiful small sacred objects. Ani-la also has gifts—tea, incense, prayer flags. I keep reminding myself to watch the time. The taxi arrives, and Oser decides to accompany me to the airport. Instead of hugging, Ani-la and I touch foreheads, as Tibetans do. Other friends have come to say goodbye and everybody is smiling and waving. I'm covered in white *katas*, grateful for all the attention and distraction from the fact that I'm actually leaving.

So here it is, my turn at departure. At the doors to the terminal, for some reason, Oser is refused entry. My need to figure things out has already vanished, as though logic has already collapsed in the face of entering thirty hours of transit regulations. I pause for a moment and in the doorway Oser and I now touch foreheads. He turns back outside and I plunge into the terminal line with my trolley of luggage.

Time seems to shift zones as I wait on line. I feel outside of its literal meaning, simply aware of its passage as a countdown to leaving behind a particular state of mind; particular to living in Boudnath, Kathmandu. I open my notebook to some lines of the late nineteenth century wandering master, Patrul Rinpoche: *"Don't prolong the past. Don't invite the future. Don't alter your innate wakefulness. Don't fear appearances."* He didn't write these words specifically about traveling, but they fit the moment perfectly.

I watch my bags clear security. I feel like these bags represent a part of me that will emerge again in another domain, another culture. *Don't invite the future.* On the next line, the one to the ticket counter, I have to step off and pay the airport tax. It costs more than the week's bill at the guest house. *Don't prolong the past.* The next hour in the waiting room upstairs, I sit and walk and imagine the stories of fellow travelers' spread out around the room. I feel at once saturated and empty. The events of the past weeks appear as stockpiles in a warehouse. I think of the monks and nuns chanting at their practice tables in the shrine room. I think of all of us inside the Guru Rinpoche cave. I hear gongs and horns and hand drums; melodies resonate in my mind. *Don't alter your innate wakefulness. Don't fear appearances.*

The red light flashes over the Singapore Airlines sign. I pick up my shoulder bag and move quickly to the exit door. I weave through the crowd telling myself, *"not too fast."* Outside on the soft tarmac of the landing field, I breathe in one last taste of hot, dusty air.

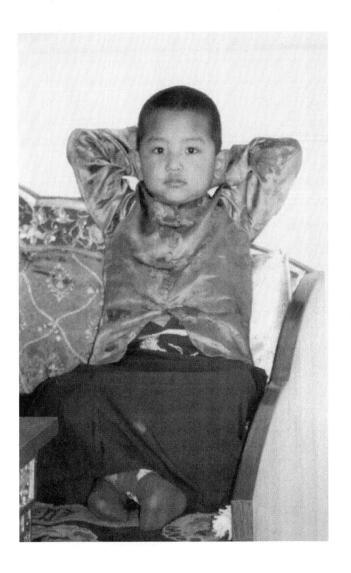

Photo Captions

About the Author

STEPHEN CLORFEINE lives in Ulster County in the Hudson Valley. He has been writing, performing, and directing theater pieces since 1975. Recent projects include, *Beginning Again*, a collection of prose poems (Advocate Press); an ongoing theatrical collaboration with actress Lanny Harrison; spoken word performances, and "Saying and Singing the Poets" with jazz singer, Jay Clayton. Stephen teaches contemplative arts workshops in the U.S. and Europe, as well as theater, poetry, and storytelling residencies in public schools. He has continued his studies and travels in both Nepal and India.

Related CD's and Cassettes by the Author

The first two chapters of this book, "Kathmandu Journal" and "Annapurna—Down the Western Slope," are available on either two CD's or two cassettes. The text is performed by the author with a soundtrack composed by Steve Gorn, the internationally renowned bamboo flutist.

The CD's are $15 each and the cassettes are $10 each, postage paid. They are available from BLUE SERGE PRODUCTIONS
Box 714 Stone Ridge, New York 12484.

The listening is an experience akin to inner pilgrimage. The dance of word, feeling and music is seamless. I know no other recording just like it.
Parabola, Summer 1999

This is an extremely engaging recording that succeeds both as a travel piece and as a portrait of the psychological and spiritual work that travel provokes.
Shambhala Sun, September 1999

...a small masterpiece of literary and musical art.
Kingston Daily Freeman, July 1999

The listener is transported by these stories, set to location recordings and soulful compositions by Steve Gorn.
Woodstock Times, August 1999